Box Kites
Making and Flying

DR BILL COCHRANE

B.T. Batsford Ltd, London

© Bill Cochrane

First published 1993

Typeset by Tek-Art Ltd, Kent

Printed in Singapore

Published by B.T. Batsford Ltd
4 Fitzhardinge Street
London W1H 0AH

British Library cataloguing-in-publication data. A catalogue record for this book is available from the British Library.

ISBN 0 7134 6920 X

Jacket illustration
Winged box kite

Page 1
Conyne kite

Metric units (millimetres) have been used for all the designs in this book. If you prefer to work in imperial units, divide the centimetre dimensions by 2·54 to convert them into inches and mark out to the nearest tenth of an inch.

CONTENTS

INTRODUCTION
THE HISTORY OF THE BOX KITE 5

ONE
WHAT IS A BOX KITE? 13

TWO
MATERIALS 21

THREE
SIMPLE BOX KITES 29

FOUR
WINGED BOX KITES 51

FIVE
FURTHER COMPOUND DESIGNS 67

FURTHER READING 94

USEFUL ADDRESSES 95

INDEX 96

INTRODUCTION

THE HISTORY OF THE BOX KITE

The kite has a long history, dating back to before the time of Christ. The exact time of its origin is rather obscure, but it is generally accepted that the kite had its beginnings in China. The first documented instance of a kite seems to have been that by General Han Hsin (d. 196 BC), who flew a kite over a palace that he wished to capture in order to ascertain the distance he needed to tunnel under it to get his troops in. The kite spread from China and was developed in the East and Far East, especially in Japan.

Lawrence Hargrave

After two thousand years, the kite took a giant leap forward when the first box kite was developed in Australia by Lawrence Hargrave. He was entranced with the idea of manned flight, and in 1893 he produced the first box kite by using two vertical surfaces or side panels to link the two horizontal lifting surfaces. The vertical panels also provided stability.

Hargrave worked on a number of designs for cellular kites, but eventually found that two simple, rectangular cells provided the best combination of lift and stability. He recognized the importance of very taut sails, and incorporated a simple but effective tensioning device. He also realized the significance of reducing the weight of his kites to a minimum and of reducing air resistance by using streamlined spars. The vertical panels provided lateral stability, halting the tendency of the kite to roll, turn from side to side or invert if the air were reduced. In the Hargrave kite the front and rear panels are separated, and this space gives fore and aft stability, reducing the tendency to dive and pitch forward and backward.

Alexander Bell

Dr Alexander Graham Bell is best remembered for inventing the electric telephone in 1876, but he also made an important contribution to aeronautical engineering. In 1893 he was apparently so impressed by a model aeroplane that he embarked on a series of experiments which he hoped would lead to manned and powered flight.

Bell took the Hargrave cellular kite as his starting point, but regarded the bracing of these kites and the wooden supports between the front and rear cells as inefficient. He designed a number of kites, including spool and radial kites. He also made a triangular box kite, a compound (multi-celled) triangular box kite, and an immensely strong and stable hexagonal box kite, which is still one of the best heavy-weather fliers.

Bell eventually settled upon tetrahedral kites (see page 11) as the most promising avenue of enquiry. He found that single tetrahedrons were not only very strong, but that if covered on two of the four sides they produced a strong and stable lift. Bell joined large numbers of tetrahedral cells together to produce some impressive structures, some of which could lift a man from the ground. He made small-scale models of his creations, using small pieces of wood or wire held together with sealing wax. When it came to building the full-sized kites, he had thousands of cells, pre-fabricated in red silk, and joined these together using universal joints made from aluminium balls with holes tapped to receive a screw thread. This meant that he could put his structures together relatively quickly and could also recycle cells from one kite to another.

Bell was ultimately faced with the problem that had thwarted Hargrave – the absence of a suitable light-weight engine to power the kites. In retrospect, the concept of a multi-celled tetrahedral kite as a vehicle for powered flight seems somewhat impracticable, but Bell's work remains a milestone in kiting history and his kites were some of the most spectacular ever made.

Charles J. Lamson

No history of the box kite would be complete without mentioning the American designer Charles J. Lamson. His interest was in man-lifting, and he built modified Hargrave kites in which control could be gained by the pilot moving the rear cell forward or backward, and sideways movement by the pilot leaning to the left or right. A similar principle is employed today in the control of some hang-gliders. Lamson developed the multi-plane folding kite in 1896, but perhaps his greatest contribution was in the production of his famous 'Aerocurve' kite in 1897. Lawrence Hargrave had applied the principle of the aerofoil – that more lift is produced when air passes over a curved surface (cambered aerofoil) than over a flat one – to some of his kites, but it was Lamson who used this to produce one of the finest kites ever made. The 'Aerocurve' represented a significant step along the road to flight.

Lawrence Hargrave and his kites (*Science Museum*)

MAN-LIFTERS AND WAR KITES

At the end of the nineteenth and beginning of the twentieth centuries, early aviation pioneers began to experiment with manned flight.

Samuel Cody

In Britain, the Baden-Powell Levitor was used for early man-lifting experiments, but the system lacked control and sophistication and was never a practicable proposition. The finest of all the man-lifting systems was developed by Samuel Franklyn Cody, one of the most colourful characters in aviation history.

Cody decided at an early stage that the box kite should be the starting point for his experiments. He began by building bigger and bigger simple box kites until he had constructed a giant kite over 27 feet high. Cody found that, as the size of a kite increases, engineering problems increase in complexity, and to overcome this he produced a double box kite with wings, to which he added points. He believed that these points improved the stability of the kite, but, even more importantly, enabled a very tense structure to be created.

Samuel Cody and a collection of his kites. These are mainly large kites, which would have been used in man-lifting trains. Note especially the very large extended-wing Cody in the background (*RAE*)

When we think of Cody today we tend to remember his war kite (see page 78), but, more significantly, he devised a system of using kites to lift relatively large weights in a controlled way (Figure 1). This involved flying a pilot kite on a length of piano wire up to a thousand feet long, to give stability and to start the process of raising the heavy steel cable upon which the rest of the kites flew. This was followed by a series of lifter kites to support the steel cable, and finally the carrier kite, which did the man-lifting. The carrier measured up to 36 feet across, and the person to be lifted aloft could control the ascent and descent of the kite via a system of bridles and levers.

Cody's ever-active mind saw other uses for his kites, including meteorological research, and in 1902 he flew his train system at Newcastle-upon-Tyne to an altitude of 14,000 feet in order to conduct studies on the upper atmosphere. In recognition of this achievement,

he was made a member of the Royal Meteorological Society. The kites used were the extended-wing Codys (see page 89), with an extra panel above the main body of the kite itself, which Cody called 'soaring kites'. This modification for high-altitude flying gave more lift and would undoubtedly have helped in gaining the altitude record.

Cody also approached the Admiralty with the suggestion that kites might be usefully employed at sea to raise observers, and for gunnery targeting, sighting submarines and signalling. He was invited to conduct trials at the naval gunnery school of HMS Excellent, situated off Portsmouth. Cody himself was lifted to a thousand feet, but this was overshadowed by the raising of Sapper Moreton to a height of 2,600 feet on the end of a cable 4,000 feet long. Despite these successes, the Admiralty turned Cody's invention down.

The Navy showed renewed interest in Cody's system in 1908, however, and a further series of trials was carried out. An excellent account of these trials can be seen in Dr Percy Walker's book, *Early Aviation at Farnborough – Balloons, Kites and Airships*. Cody also pushed on with his dream of powered flight, and in October of that year he achieved the first powered flight in Britain, which lasted for 27 seconds and covered a distance of 1,390 feet.

The Wright brothers

In recent years four-line-control kites have become popular, but the first of these were made almost a century earlier by the Wright brothers, as part of the project which would ultimately lead to the development of the first powered aeroplane. Like other early aviators, the Wright brothers seem to have taken the flight of birds as their starting point.

They noted that, when birds wished to manoeuvre, they altered the shape of their wings and, as a result, they built a steerable glider in 1899 which could be controlled by 'warping' the wings. This was a biplane kite, in which the wings were warped up or down by means of two pairs of control lines. At each side, one line was attached to the upper corner of the wing with the other attached to the lower corner.

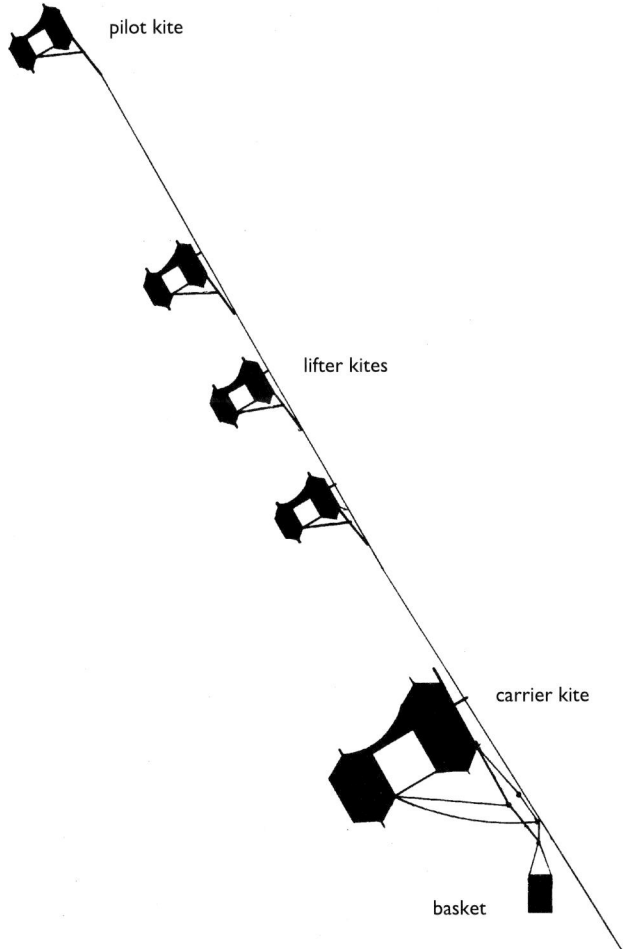

pilot kite

lifter kites

carrier kite

basket

1   Cody's system for a man-lifting train of war kites

Man-lift carried out during naval trials, 1903 (*RAE*)

KITES AND METEOROLOGICAL RESEARCH

In the early days of atmospheric exploration, information was gathered by balloons and kites. Perhaps the most spectacular research was that undertaken to investigate electrical discharges, using 'electric kites'. In the eighteenth century, Benjamin Franklin constructed a simple kite from a silk handkerchief and cedar spars, and discovered that, when the kite was flown in a thunderstorm, electrical currents passed down the damp kite line and were discharged through a metal key. Similar experiments were performed by a French scientist called de Romas, who claimed to have produced sparks up to 18 feet long.

Early atmospheric experiments, using kites to lift recording instruments, were carried out in England by W.R. Birt in 1847, but it was not until the latter part of the nineteenth century that kite technology could provide a sufficiently stable lifting system for recording instruments. In the 1890s two very stable, tail-less kites were developed: the Eddy bowed kite and the Hargrave box kite, together with lightweight measuring instruments. In 1894, a train of five Eddy kites lifted automatic recording instruments weighing two-and-a-quarter pounds (1 kg) to a height of 14,000 feet, but these were superseded by Hargrave-type cellular kites, often flown in trains on several miles of high-tensile steel wire. It should be noted that flying kites on metal wire is extremely dangerous, with up to 50,000 volts being recorded. Electric shocks were apparently not unusual, and at least one person was killed during these experiments.

The development of the aeroplane made meteorological observation by kites redundant, and the last United States Weather Bureau station closed in 1933.

BARRAGE KITES

With the advent of powered flight, the impetus to develop kites as part of mainstream technology had gone, but the Second World War brought renewed interest in them as a way of protecting shipping from marauding aircraft. In the United States, large, commercial box kites used for advertising were modified to produce barrage kites which could be used to protect ships, particularly from dive-bombers. The naval barrage kite was about six metres wide and could be flown on long wire lines, which were capable of fouling propellors and cutting wings from aircraft. A system developed in Britain employed an ingenious mechanical device in which the impact of an enemy plane on the flying line of the kite caused the bomb to be armed and drawn up the kite line, to explode on impact with the enemy plane.

Interest also revived in the Cody kite as a barrage kite in the years prior to the Second World War. A small batch of Cody kites was re-created at Farnborough, and a further batch of approximately two thousand was produced by a contractor. Some of these replicas have survived and can be seen in museums as specimens of a Cody kite.

Another use for box kites at this time was as an aid in the recovery of airmen who had ditched their planes at sea. The best-known of these was the Gibson Girl rescue kite, used to raise radio aerials. This was an ingenious little kite – compact, easily erected and stable in flight – with an aluminium frame and a strong yellow-fabric covering. When the pilot had landed in the sea, he could fly the kite from his position in the waves. It was flown on edge from one of two towing points (depending on wind conditions) from a steel cable. The cable acted not only as a line for the kite, but also as a radio aerial. Over 20,000 of these kites were made, and many survive to this day.

BOX KITES FOR PLEASURE AND LEISURE

Today many types of cellular kite are flown for their aerial spectacle. The fact that classic kites such as the Cody remain popular today – almost a century after they were designed and developed – is a testimony to their quality, but exciting designs continue to emerge.

New materials such as ripstop nylon, fibreglass and carbon fibre (see pages 22–5) have enhanced the performance of some early kites, and other changes have been made, such as the addition of delta wings to Conyne kites and winged box kites to increase performance in light winds. The opportunity of utilizing modern materials to produce striking visual effects has also been exploited, resulting in exceptionally attractive kites with sparkling performance such as the Peter Lynn Tri-D box kite (see page 63).

Bell's tetrahedral kites (see right) continue to attract the interest of kite-makers throughout the world, and some very attractive multi-coloured examples have been produced. For a kite to be useful today, however, it needs to be portable and easy to assemble, and this has been a great drawback with this type of kite. Some

commercially produced universal-jointing systems have been developed, but most of these are somewhat flimsy and can be tricky to use.

One of the most popular and innovative modern designs is the 'Professor Waldorf' box kite, designed by Peter Waldren. It consists of a front and a rear cell, linked by triangular wings. Each of these is made up of hexagonal cells, joined to smaller internal cells by rectangular panels. The kite is erected via diagonal spars, and several can be flown in a larger assembly to make a spectacular aerial sculpture (see page 19).

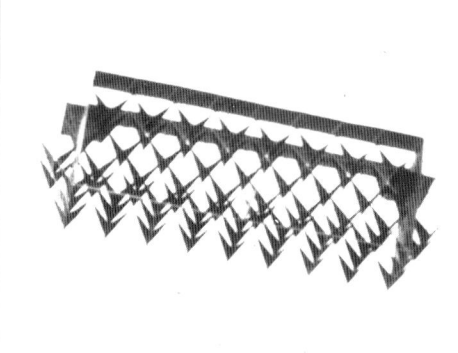

Alexander Bell's large, multi-celled tetrahedral kite in flight (*Library of Congress collection*)

OTHER CELLULAR KITES

Facet kites (with the frame on the outside) represent an interesting extension of the box kite, but perhaps the ultimate cellular kite is the parafoil. Hargrave experimented with a single-celled box kite with an aerofoil section, but it was not until 1963 that Domina Jalbert developed the first parafoil.

The parafoil has no solid structural elements, but consists of a number of cells separated by vertical risers. Each cell has a vent at the leading edge of the kite, so that, as air enters the cells, the whole structure inflates to produce the aerofoil section. Beneath the aerofoil wing are fins which keep the kite facing into the wind. This is essential as, once the wind ceases to enter the aerofoil, the wing collapses.

The original parafoil has now been further developed to try to eradicate the tendency to deflate. Valves have been installed to control the entry of the air, and also to regulate the loss of air, so that if the wind is lost the deflation of the aerofoil shape is not so dramatic, giving time for recovery. With kites of this type, most of the lift is developed at the leading edge, so that its design is critical.

Another development of the air-filled wing was the flexifoil, a flexible wing braced at the leading edge by a fibreglass or carbon-fibre spar, and flown on dual-control lines. Air is admitted through net strips across the leading edge. Flexifoils give sparkling performance and are not only amongst the fastest of all kites but are also very manoeuvrable. Individual flexifoils give tremendous pull for their size, but a stack of them generates heart-stopping performance.

Some of the most original and interesting of the novelty type of box kites are those produced by the Dutch kite-makers Jan Pieter Kuil and Janne van Nederpelt. They make a wide range of kites which are characterized by their superb design and construction. Included in their collection are unique flying models of castles, trains, cars, lorries and so on (see page 17). These are all constructed using thin dowel and joints made of thermoplastic tubing, and illustrate the scope that box and cellular kites offer to the imaginative kite-maker. Despite the relatively simple nature of their construction, these kites fly incredibly well and are a star attraction at kite festivals wherever they are flown.

Parafoil

ONE

WHAT IS A BOX KITE?

A box kite is a kite which has a box section or cellular structure, and therefore has three or more sides (Figure 2). To increase performance, wings are often added to the basic box section to produce compound box kites. Fashions in kite-making come and go, but the popularity of the box kite has endured to the present day. There is an extensive range of these kites, and they are ideal for all children between the ages of five and 99! Kites today are seen as a source of fun and entertainment, but, as we have seen, the box kite started off as a serious scientific experiment to find a lifting device that would eventually lead to powered flight.

The discovery of the box kite is credited to Lawrence Hargrave in the 1890s (see page 6), although much of its subsequent development has taken place in Europe and North America. Many of the box kites flown today were designed in the early part of the twentieth century, or are modern adaptations of early designs. The early kite-fliers were not the amateurs we see today but dedicated scientists and technologists. It is perhaps not surprising that some of the designs created around the end of the last century were so good that they have been difficult to improve on.

To understand why men of such calibre were building kites it is necessary to look back at the times in which they were living. Powered flight, which had been man's dream for centuries, was within their grasp and the development of the kite was a focus for scientific and technological research. In searching for a design which would allow manned flight, the early pioneers were looking for a light, strong structure which would give stable and predictable flight in a variety of wind conditions. These are still the ideal characteristics for kites today.

Box kites have great natural stability and adapt better to gusty and unpredictable wind patterns than most other types of kite. This inherent stability is particularly useful when flying a train of kites, as tails can present problems when several kites are flown together on one line. By adopting well-thought-out construction techniques it is possible to have more than one set of spars for each box kite, so that a light set can be selected for light wind conditions and a heavier set for windier conditions. With carefully chosen combinations of spars and bridle settings, box kites can therefore be flown on more days in the year than any other type of kite.

Box kites have a three-dimensional structure which enables them to 'fill the sky', and they can be a very impressive sight, with plenty of scope for different colour combinations and innovative design. Traditionally, box kites have had triangular or rectangular box sections, but many striking kites based on hexagons, such as the 'Professor Waldorf' kite, have been produced.

2   Anatomy of a box kite

THE KITE AND THE WIND

There are three factors to consider when thinking about the wind: its speed, its quality, and its turbulence at ground level.

Wind speed

The speed of the wind can be accurately measured with an anemometer, or estimated using the Beauford scale (see overleaf). The Beauford scale gives the speed of the wind at ground level, but this could well be higher at the kite's flying altitude. This is an important factor when deciding whether a kite should be flown in certain conditions.

Winerack Kite

Sutton Flowform

Wind quality

The quality of the wind is more difficult to evaluate, as there are several factors to be taken into account. Sometimes there is a steady breeze, ideal for flying kites, but at other times there may be continual variations in wind speed. This can be dangerous when there are strong gusts or squalls, as sudden surges in wind speed can produce large increases in lift, snapping lines and causing damage to kites.

Cody train

Shortened Beauford scale

Note: the full scale goes to force 12 and contains much more detail.

Wind type	Speed (m.p.h.)	Beauford number and effects
Calm	1	0 Calm air, smoke rises vertically
Light air	2-3	1 Smoke drifts gently showing wind direction
Light breeze	4-7	2 Wind felt on face, leaves rustle
Gentle breeze	8-12	3 Leaves and small twigs on trees move
Moderate breeze	13-18	4 Dust rises, small branches move
Fresh breeze	19–24	5 Small trees in leaf sway
Strong breeze	25–31	6 Large branches move and kite-flying becomes dangerous

Ground turbulence

The conditions at ground level are often the most difficult that a kite will encounter, and most damage occurs at take-off and landing. Kites which are stable at altitude may not fare well in turbulent conditions at ground level, and an additional stabilizing device such as a drogue can sometimes be used. Most box kites can be flown in fairly strong breezes, but, by using lighter spars and lightweight fabric, it is also possible to produce box kites which will fly in relatively light winds.

Some box kites are designed to fly in extremely strong winds. Early this century, Cody made kites with spars of thick bamboo, which, it was claimed, could lift a man safely in wind speeds of up to 70 m.p.h. There are few people today who would wish to fly a kite in that type of wind, let alone be lifted up on one.

Delta Conyne

WHY DO KITES FLY?

When a gale is blowing, it is common to hear people say that it is 'good weather for flying kites'. In fact, nothing could be further from the truth. Well-made kites will fly in winds which are much less than a gale, and the problem is often not how to get them up, but how to get them down. In the air, kites experience the forces of lift, drag and gravity.

Lift

When a kite is held at a suitable angle into the wind, the force of the wind against the kite sail creates an upward force called *lift*. The separation of the airflow over the kite surface creates differences in pressure. A kite is not only pushed upwards by the lift on the underside of the wing (the kite face), but is to a lesser extent sucked upwards by the partial vacuum on its upper surface (back). The centre of lift is the point on the kite face which is the focal point of the forces of lift.

Train kite by Jan Pieter Kuil and Janne van Nederpelt

Drag

The force of *drag*, created as the wind flows over the kite, is due to the difference in pressure between the upper and lower surfaces and friction drag. Drag acts against the force of lift, but is essential for stability. Sometimes the kite may not produce sufficient drag to allow stable flight, and a drag-inducing device such as a drogue or tail is used. The centre of drag is the point on the kite face where the forces of drag seem to act.

Gravity

Gravity is the force which pulls a kite down to earth. The lighter a kite is, the less the force of gravity on it will be. The centre of gravity is the point at which the force of gravity seems to act on the kite.

Centre of pressure

Lift, drag and gravity all balance at a point on the kite face called the *centre of pressure*. The kite line needs to pass through or above the centre of pressure to fly successfully (Figure 3). This can be achieved by tying the line to the kite face at an appropriate point, but is more often attained by means of a bridle. The force which holds the kite in the air is the tension which exists in the kite line. If there is no tension, a kite cannot fly.

The pressure on the kite face which produces lift can be altered by adjusting the angle of the bridle, or by moving the point of attachment along the kite if the line is attached directly to the kite. When suspended upside-down from the bridling point, the kite should make an angle of between 20-30° with the ground. The bridle can be adjusted to compensate for the wind speed. As the speed of the wind increases, the angle of attack formed by the bridle is decreased. The length of the bridle lines can vary, but, generally, longer bridle lines give more even flight.

In practical terms, it is difficult to give exact bridle settings for any kite, as these depend on characteristics unique to each kite and on the conditions in which it is being flown. In view of this, any bridle measurements given in this book are a rough guide only, and you may find it preferable to determine your own, unique bridle point. As a general rule, the towing point (the point at which the bridle meets the flying line) is situated about one third of the way down the spine from the front and about half the length of the kite from the lower kite face.

With some box kites, there is no need to worry about adjusting the bridle. If it is flown on edge, the flying line can be attached directly to the kite one third of the way down the spine. To fly the kite flat, simply fix a length of flying line approximately three metres long across the two front lower corners and form a loop at the mid-point. Attach the flying line to the loop and the kite will find its own best angle of flight and will, incidentally, give a relatively light pull. See Figure 9 on page 33 for bridling suggestions for a simple box kite.

The triangular elements of the box sections give some lift and stability (Figure 4). When wings are added, they increase lift by providing horizontal surfaces (Figure 5, overleaf). However, in producing lift, the drag can be reduced. In a light wind, the extra lift may be useful, but in a stronger wind it may lead to instability. One way to tackle this may be to change the angle of attack, but another avenue to explore is to bow the wing. This alters the wings from a flat surface providing only lift to an angled dihedral surface. In strong winds it can be useful to alter the angle of attack and to bow the spar supporting the wings. This is perhaps one of the areas where the skill of the kite-flier is really important – that is, to be able to adjust the kite so that it will fly in a range of flying conditions. The range of wind speeds in which a kite will fly is sometimes called the 'flying window'.

For a square or rectangular box kite, flown flat to the wind, the horizontal surfaces produce lift with the vertical ones providing stability. Angled wings (as seen, for example, in most of the winged compound kites) give extra lift, which greatly increases their performance. Of course, if the wings are too big, the extra lift can lead to instability.

In some box kites the shape is maintained by the upward pressure of the kite against the tow line. This is the principle employed in some types of triangular kite and compound variations such as the well-known Conyne kite. The advantage of maintaining cell shape in

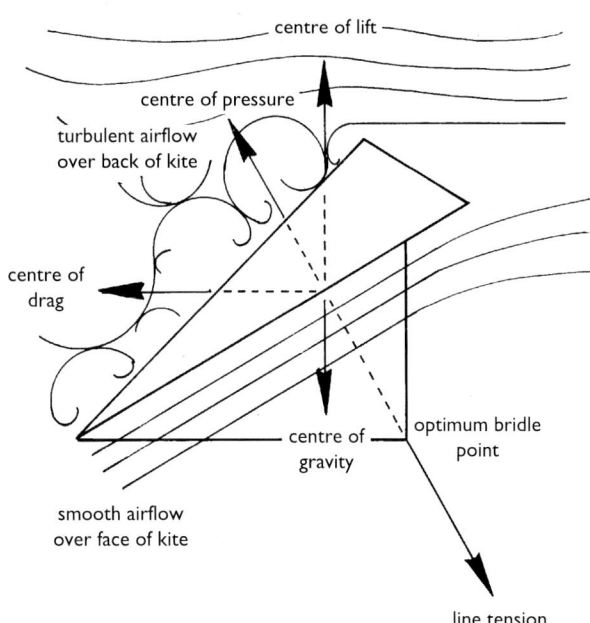

3   Diagram showing the various forces experienced by a kite when flown

**Eight-unit Waldorf assembly
made by Peter Waldren**

**4   Stability and lift in a simple
box kite: (a) square box flown
flat: horizontal sides give lift,
vertical sides give stability
(b) square box flown on edge:
all sides give lift and stability
(c) triangular box: horizontal
(top) side gives lift, triangular
sides give lift and stability**

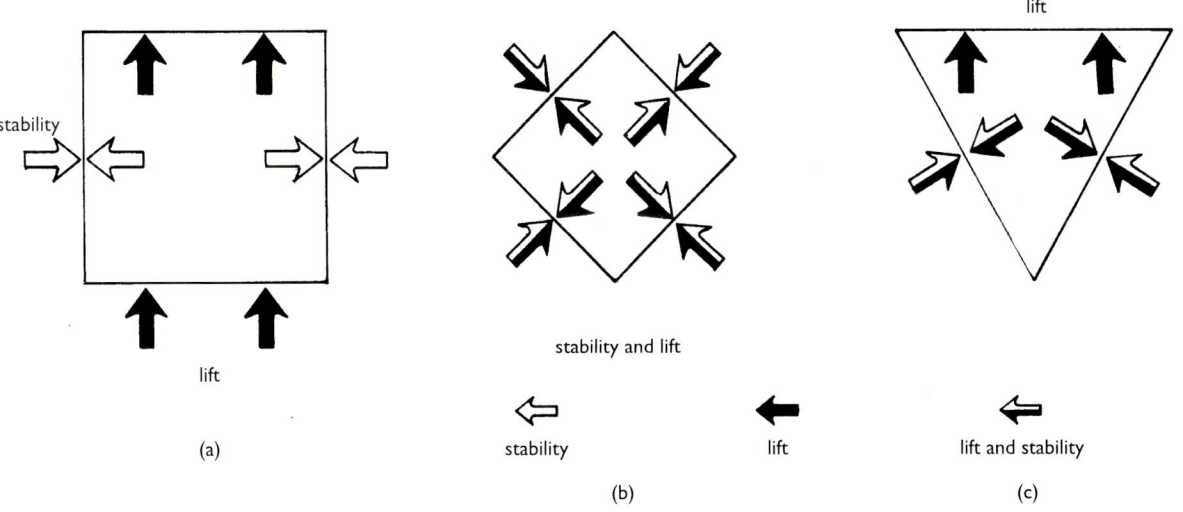

this way is that it makes construction easier and also represents a saving in weight. The principle is quite successful, but seems to lack the stabilizing power of rigidly maintained sections. Some Conyne kites seem to suffer from a degree of flapping in the rear cell, but paradoxically this appears to lead to stability – presumably by inducing an extra degree of drag. The Conynes have good stability in steady winds, but gusty side winds appear to distort the shapes of the cells with a concomitant loss of stability. The Conyne, incidentally, is a high-performance kite which sometimes tends to over-perform in high winds when made of ripstop nylon. It is a much better-behaved and more forgiving kite when made of cotton like the originals.

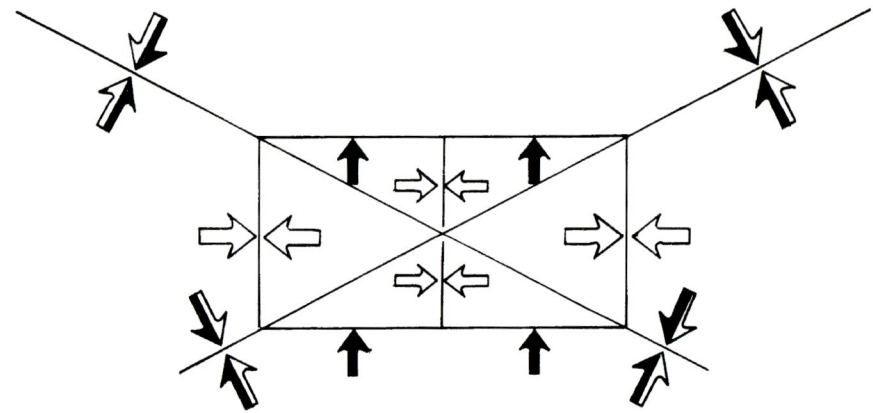

5   Stability and lift in a compound box kite

Cody kite by Paul Chapman

Rigid cells, maintained by some form of bracing, give the greatest degree of stability, since their integrity is not dependent upon the wind. Their construction can, however, pose considerable technical problems, as well as incurring weight penalties. There are several methods of creating a rigid cell, and if a structure does not have to be collapsible, the problems can be more easily overcome. Collapsible kites clearly have many advantages, and most kites can be broken down for easy storage and transport. Even large box kites can be constructed in such a way that they can be easily transported. In order to maintain the box sections, there have traditionally been two approaches: first, to brace from inside the box sections so that the cells are pushed out, and secondly, to have spars projecting outside the cells and attached in such a way that the cells are pulled outward. An alternative is to put the whole frame on the outside to pull the cells outward, as in facet kites.

To increase performance, wings may be added to produce compound box kites which have both high stability and high performance. These have tended to be relatively small, in order that the structural integrity is not compromised and that the extra lift does not exceed the stabilizing capacity of the vertical elements of the box sections. A departure from this has been the development of the delta box kite, in which the triangular box sections provide stability to complement the considerable performance of the semi-flexible delta wing. The delta wing also provides extra stability so that the kite remains balanced even with the larger wing.

TWO
MATERIALS

When making a box kite it will be necessary to select materials for the sails, and for the spars which give the kite its shape. It is also worth giving some thought to the pull which the completed kite will develop and to the line which will be needed to fly it safely.

SAIL MATERIALS

The traditional materials for box-kite construction are fabric and hardwood. The first box kites were developed at the end of the nineteenth century, and fabrics chosen by the pioneers included cotton cambric (a finely woven fabric), sailcloth and silk.

Cloth

Cloth is still the predominant material used in the sails of box kites today. By their very nature, box kites are relatively heavy and tend to be flown in breezier conditions than lightweight kites such as delta kites and flares. They therefore need a robust construction,

making cloth the most suitable material for the sails. The early makers of box kites soon realized that one of the most important features of the sails was that they had to be extremely taut, putting them under considerable pressure. For many box kites, therefore, materials with little structural strength, such as paper, are unsuitable.

An important but often overlooked point about cotton as a kite-making fabric is that a certain degree of inherent lift regulation is associated with porous fabrics. This is because, as the wind speed increases, more wind is forced through the cloth. This degree of self-regulation brings more porous fabrics into their own in very strong winds.

Ripstop nylon

Natural fabrics such as cotton cambric and silk have been replaced by ripstop nylon as the first choice for most kite-making. Ripstop nylon is light, very strong, and virtually impervious to the wind due to a surface coating of PVC (polyvinyl chloride). It is also relatively easy to work with, comes in a dazzling array of colours and is fairly cheap. Ripstop nylon does not fray when

Cross-joint formed using 'O' ring

Cross-joint formed by lashing

Cross-joint formed from drilled plastic tubing. If aluminium tubing is used instead, it should be drilled and positioned in exactly the same way

Right-angle joint formed from lashed plastic tubing

Right-angle joint formed from drilled aluminium tubing

Right-angle joint formed from lashed wooden supports

cut, and this clearly sets it on its own as a fabric for kite construction. (It is possible to make kites without hems around the edges, but generally it is better to use a narrow seam.)

There are several types of ripstop nylon available, with variations in weight and feel, but they all have the same basic properties. For heavy-duty work, spinnaker nylon is ideal, but it has a slight weight disadvantage and is more expensive than thinner ripstop.

Polythene

Polythene sheet has some useful properties, such as being impervious to wind, but its applications are somewhat limited as it is a difficult material to work with and cannot be glued, leaving adhesive tape as the only practical way of joining it. It also tends to stretch easily, and, as box kites have sails under tension, this is a serious drawback.

Polyester film

Polyester films such as Mylar or Mellinex can be quite useful in small-scale applications, and can be readily purchased in the form of rolls of 'wrapping-paper'. Some synthetic papers can also be used because they are much stronger than ordinary paper, and materials such as Synteape can be painted or drawn on. Due to the stress encountered in box-kite sails, glued kites do not tend to have a very long life, so it comes down to sewing.

SPARS

There is a choice of materials for the spars of a box kite. It is not always a good idea to have spars that are too strong, as when a kite crashes it is useful to have a weak point in the kite which will 'give'. If the weak point is a wooden spar, then the kite can usually be fairly easily repaired. However, if virtually unbreakable materials such as fibreglass are used, then it will be the fabric that is damaged. There is also the safety aspect

Notched end of spar protected by lashing. If tape is used instead, it should be positioned in exactly the same way

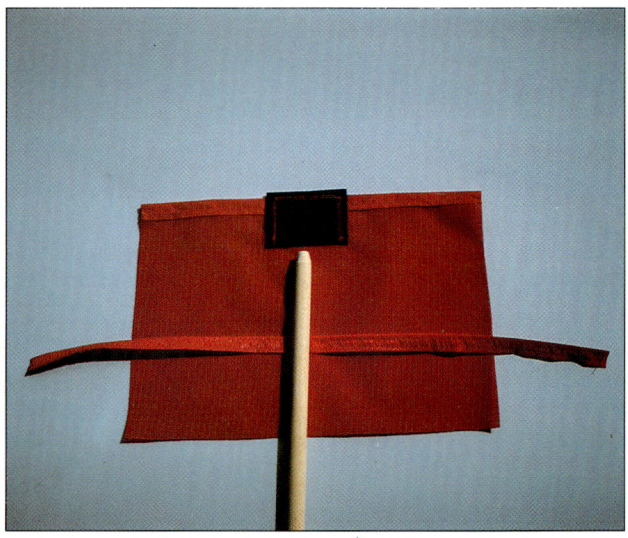

Dacron pocket and tape tie with spar being inserted

Fully assembled pocket

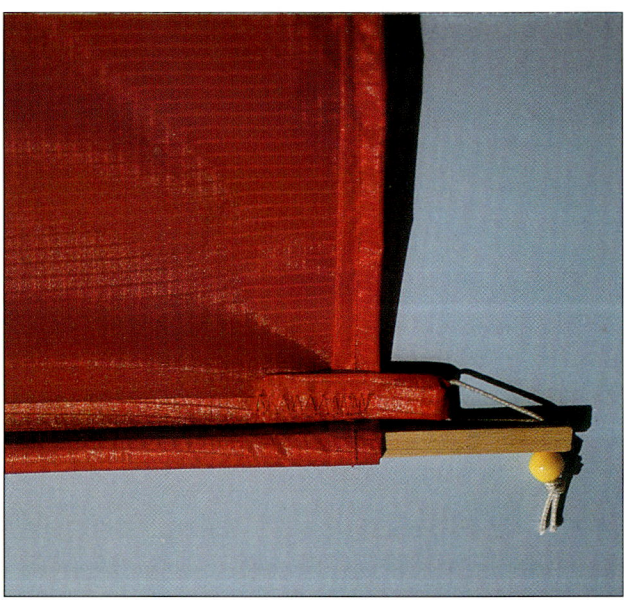

Spar secured by notch and bead at end of pocket

Multiple-bead system used at end of wing, showing arrangement of reinforced tip, tape loop and beads with spar in place

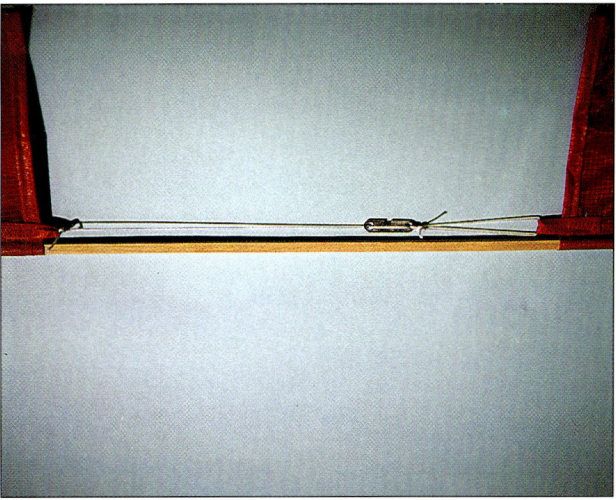

Method of keeping cells together by means of internal tape loops, linked by a line fitted with an adjustable bow tensioner. Bracing lines may be used as an alternative to the tensioner

to be considered. Strong materials such as fibreglass, carbon fibre and aluminium tubing could cause severe damage to people or property, whereas wood is safer because it lacks the strength of these materials.

Hardwood

Hardwood is still the most preferred material for con-structing spars, being easy and safe to work with and relatively strong. It comes in a variety of prepared shapes such as dowel, square section and strip.

Fibreglass

Fibreglass, also known as GRP (glass-reinforced plastic), in the form of a rod or tube is virtually unbreakable, but tends to bend, imposing some limitations on its use as a bracing material. There are also some problems associated with its use, and the dust produced when it is sawn is harmful. When working with fibreglass, it is best to cut it out of doors and to use a face mask. There can also be fine splinters from the surface which can get into the fingers, so it is a good idea to give fibreglass a coating of a polyurethane varnish to prevent this. Fibreglass is also very abrasive and quickly cuts through pockets, so the ends need to be covered with a rubber end cap. If you wish to use the bead-and-notch system suggested for many of the kites in

this book, you will need to glue an arrow nock to the end of the fibreglass (see overleaf), as notching can cause it to split.

Carbon fibre

Carbon fibre is now becoming more widely available, and is often found in high-performance stunt kites. It has great strength and is relatively light. Its application is basically that of fibreglass, but it is generally a superior product, although more expensive.

Aluminium alloy

Aluminium alloy can be used for spars, but it can become a very dangerous structure if it crashes. It will also make the kite appear on airport radar systems. Alloy tubing is very expensive, and its main applications are therefore for jointing wooden spars.

Bamboo

Bamboo is an excellent material for use in box kites. However, it is quite difficult finding bamboo with a strong and relatively even structure which is free from splits and other breaks. The type found in garden centres tends to be of very poor quality and is unsuit-able for kite-making.

FLYING LINE

Box kites tend to be flown in stronger winds and can therefore be expected to give a greater pull than some other types of kite. This means that the line used to fly them will need to have reasonable strength. Most kite line will have had its breaking strain tested and a figure will be given in pounds or kilograms.

It is important to use a line which is suitable for the kite you are flying. If you use a line which is too light, clearly there will be the possibility of it breaking, and if you use a line which is far too heavy, the kite will not fly very well because of the weight of line that it has to lift.

As a general rule, a safe margin is to allow 20 kg for each square metre of sail area (5 pounds per square foot). It can be useful to measure the pull that the kite actually gives with a spring balance and then to base the strength of line on the figure obtained, but include a generous safety margin to allow for gusts, weakening due to knots and so on.

There is a wide choice of types of line available, but generally a good-quality braided polyester or dacron is suitable. Some of the high-cost, low-stretch, lightweight lines are perhaps worth buying for stunt kites, but the expense of this line is not usually justified for box kites.

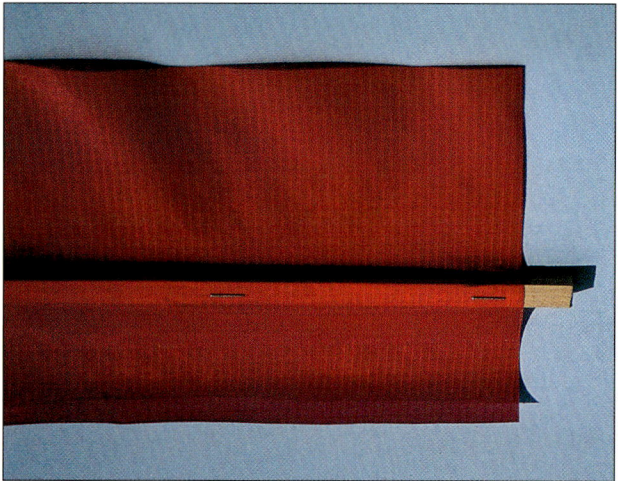

Quick and easy method of securing cell to square-section longeron using staples

Line storage

You will also need a line-storage system. Cody used a winch for his kites, but he flew them on steel cable, and his line was robust enough to take this rough treatment. If a stretched line is wound on to a reel or winch enormous pressures are created, which can damage the line or the reel. It is best to regard reels and winders as line-storage systems, rather than line-retrieval systems. Any of the popular line-storage systems such as yo-yo reels, fishing reels and wooden winders are generally suitable.

For most of the kites described in this book, box sections in the region of 400 mm (16 ins) have been used. These produce kites of a reasonable size, which fly well on relatively light line (100–150 pounds [50–75 kg] breaking strain). Kites of this size can generally be constructed with a frame of 6–9 mm ($^1/_4$–$^3/_8$ in) hardwood dowel, but for larger kites, thicker timber will need to be used.

Use of an arrow nock as an alternative to notching dowel or fibreglass. The end of the spar is semi-sharpened with a pencil sharpener and the arrow nock is glued in place

METHODS

Sewing need not be daunting when using ripstop nylon, because it is relatively easy to work with and does not fray. Marking out can be done with tailor's chalk, but the line tends to be too thick and can be rubbed out, so a soft pencil sometimes comes in useful. Tacking can usually be dispensed with; instead, the ripstop can be held in place with stick or impact adhesive. Stick adhesives can generally be removed by washing the completed kite in warm water, and impact adhesives can add to the overall strength of the kite. Other fabrics can also be used to good effect, but they are more difficult to work with and tend to be more expensive than ripstop nylon. Porous fabrics can be good in very gusty conditions (see page 22), and if a traditional box kite is made from ripstop and its flight is not completely satisfactory, it might be worth considering the possibility that the choice of fabric may be responsible.

Decorative techniques

The box-kite pioneers built their kites as strictly functional pieces of scientific equipment. Today, kites are often built to be visually attractive. Ripstop nylon is an excellent material, but is unfortunately resistant to surface paints and dyes. To create colour spectacles, other decorative techniques are therefore often necessary. One of the simplest is to stitch sections of ripstop of different colours together in panels. Appliqué is another popular technique. Cut-away appliqué is particularly effective when the background colour is white and cut away, rather than when the underlying colour is darker. In surface appliqué, pieces of material can be affixed to the surface with a stick adhesive before being stitched in place.

Typical application of yacht shackle: strong and easy to use

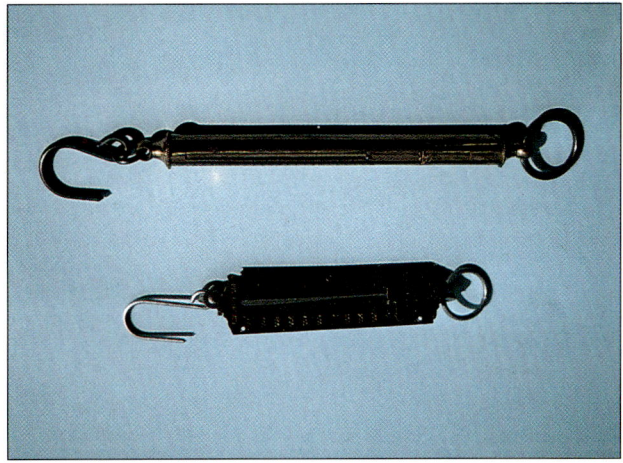

Large and small spring balances, used to determine line tension

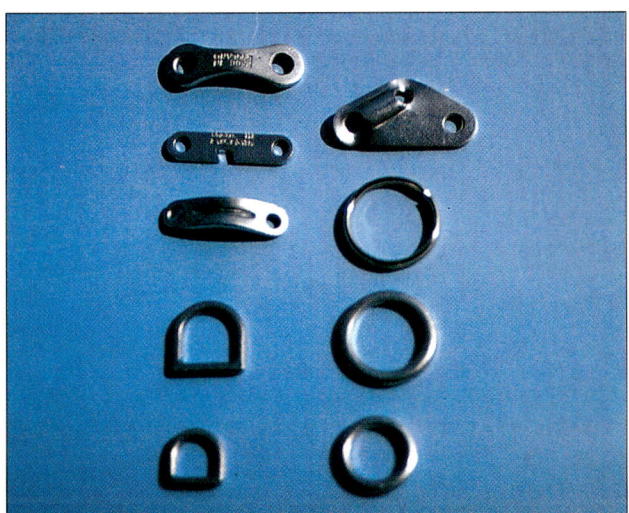

Variety of aluminium fittings used in kite-making: bow adjusters, D-rings and circular rings of different sizes

Lark's-head hitch knot, used to fasten flying line to ring

Round-turn and two half-hitch knots, used to secure a line or rope to a spar

Reef knot, used to join two lengths of line

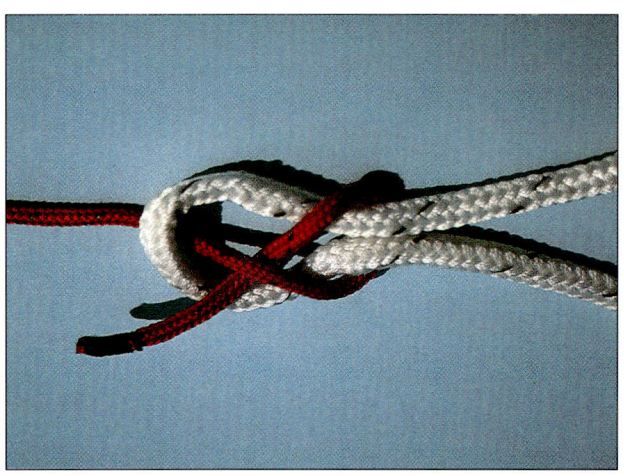

Double-sheet bend, used to join two lengths of line of differing size

Rolling-hitch knot on a rail

THREE

SIMPLE BOX KITES

SIMPLE BOX KITE
MADE FROM HARDWOOD AND PLASTIC SHEETING

A simple box kite is a box kite which does not have any wings as additional lifting surfaces. Box kites of this type can be made in a variety of sizes, from small to large. The production of a simple box kite can be complicated by the need to develop a jointing system. Joints involving cutting out parts of the spar are generally inadvisable because they weaken the spars. Those involving metals other than aluminium are too heavy, and aluminium, as well as being expensive, cannot be easily welded or brazed. For small kites, however, easy joints can be made with plastic tubing.

The best kites are generally made from cloth, but small box kites can be very successfully constructed with polythene, mylar or paper sails. One simple method is to fabricate the framework, and then to secure the sail material to it using adhesive tape or staples.

Small box kites need not be made so that they will fold up, but larger ones will need to be collapsible for easy transport and storage.

A simple box kite made from fabric and braced by diagonal spars

The usual way to collapse a box kite is to remove the cross-spars. The longerons of box kites often protrude slightly beyond the sails to protect the sails, and also to give an easy point to which the bridle can be attached.

MATERIALS

○ Polythene, mylar or paper: two pieces 1660 x 400 mm
○ Longerons: hardwood dowel, four pieces 6 x 1240 mm
○ Cross-spars: hardwood dowel, eight pieces 6 x 565 mm long
○ Thermoplastic tubing (such as motor-car fuel line): internal diameter 6 mm, length 800 mm
○ PVA glue and adhesive tape
○ Aluminium ring for bridling point

METHOD

Note:
The structure of this kite is the same as the Rainbow kite, shown on pages 35–7.

1   On each length of dowel, make a mark 20 mm and 420 mm from each end. These lines represent the points at which the joints will be fixed, 10 mm from the edge of each sail. Next, cut sixteen pieces of thermoplastic tubing, each 50 mm long. These will be used to make the joints for the cross-spars.

2   There are several simple ways in which these joints can be made (Figure 6a–c). Perhaps the simplest is to make a hole 6 mm in diameter, close to one end of the tubing, so that the longeron will pass through this hole but will be a tight fit. A hot soldering iron can be used to melt a suitable hole, but the fumes produced are not very pleasant, and this is a job best done out of doors.

An alternative is to use a cork borer to cut through the tube, or to drill holes. To make drilling easier, push a piece of dowel into the tube, clamp the tube in a vice and drill through the tube and the dowel, then push the dowel out. When the joints have been made they can be pushed on to the longerons. Another option is to make a longitudinal cut halfway through the tube for half its length, and then to open out the cut tube which can be glued and lashed to the longerons.

6a–c   Use of plastic tubing to create joints

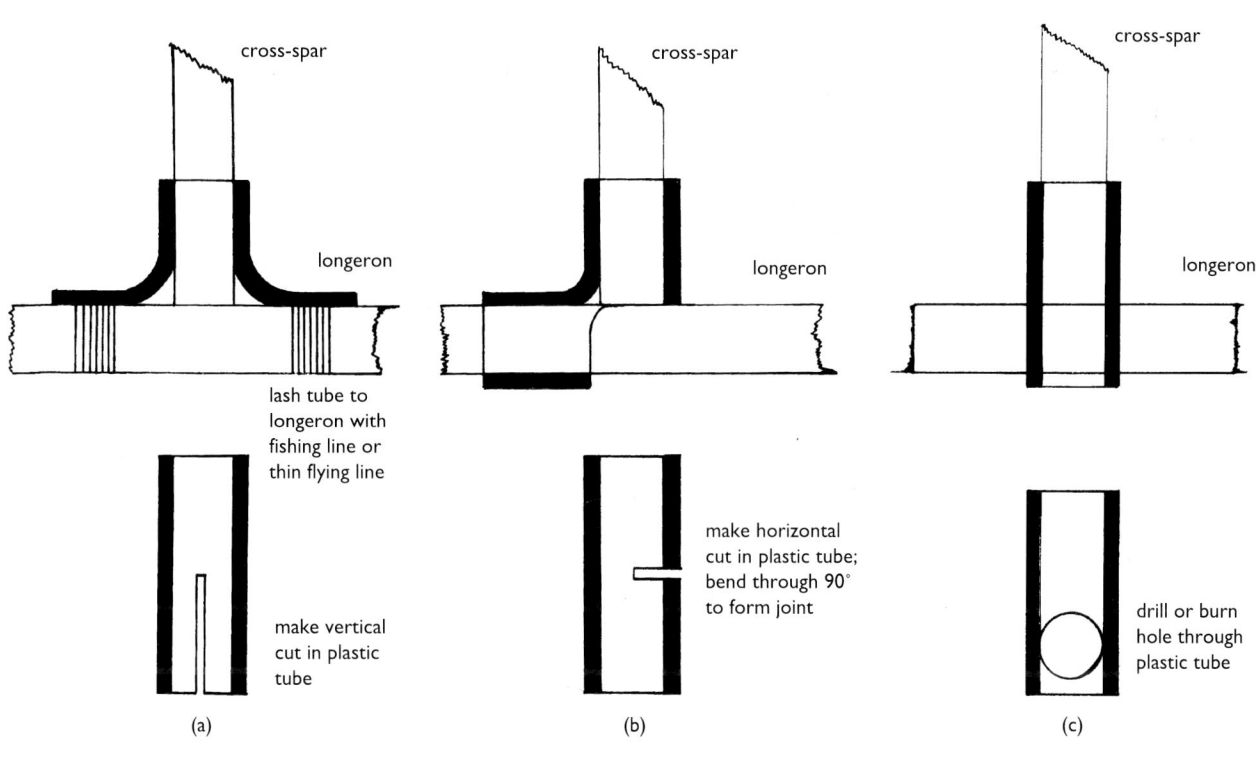

cross-spar

longeron

lash tube to longeron with fishing line or thin flying line

make vertical cut in plastic tube

(a)

cross-spar

longeron

make horizontal cut in plastic tube; bend through 90° to form joint

(b)

cross-spar

longeron

drill or burn hole through plastic tube

(c)

3 Whichever method is chosen, fit the joints to the longerons and assemble the framework by pushing the cross-spars into the plastic joints. Where the cross-spars meet, tie them tightly together with a piece of flying line to create a rigid frame (Figure 7).

4 The next stage is to fit the covering. This can be a single length of sail covering, or individual panels. Mark out two strips of polythene sheet, mylar or paper 1660 mm long and 400 mm wide. Starting at one edge of the frame, wrap the 20 mm allowance at one end of a strip around the longeron 20 mm from the end and stick down with glue or adhesive tape. Stretch the polythene sheeting or paper on to the frame to give rigid panels, and complete the box section by gluing or taping the 20 mm allowance to the last panel. Repeat with the second piece. Secure the sails to the inside of the longeron with adhesive tape. The completed structure is shown in Figure 8.

5 This kite can be bridled in several ways: see Figure 9. Tie the line to the longerons, making small holes in the fabric if necessary. The line should have a breaking strain of 35 kg (70 lb).

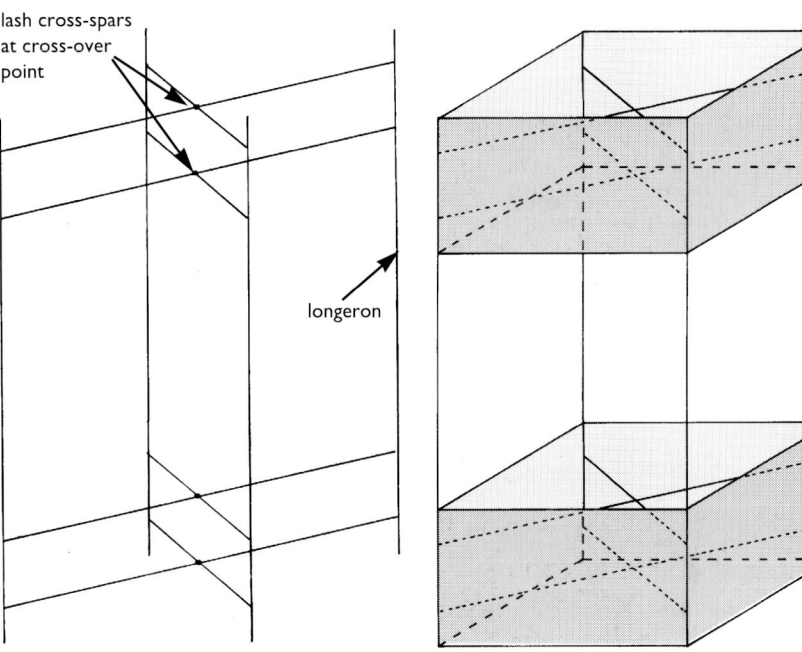

lash cross-spars at cross-over point

longeron

7   Framework for a box kite   **8   Completed box kite**

SIMPLE BOX KITE
MADE FROM FABRIC

Kites made from paper, mylar and plastic sheeting can be produced relatively quickly and inexpensively, but unfortunately their life span is also relatively short. A kite will last longer if it is constructed from cloth. Ripstop nylon is the kite-maker's favourite fabric, but other lightweight fabrics can also be used. Cloth kites can generally be made larger than their paper or plastic counterparts.

MATERIALS

○ Ripstop nylon or other fabric: two pieces 1610 x 410 mm
○ Longerons: hardwood dowel, four pieces 6 x124 mm
○ Cross-spars: hardwood dowel, eight pieces 6 x 565 mm
○ Thermoplastic tubing: internal diameter 6 mm, length 480 mm
○ Cardboard
○ Staple gun
○ Aluminium ring for bridling point

9   Bridling suggestions for flying a simple box kite (see text overleaf)

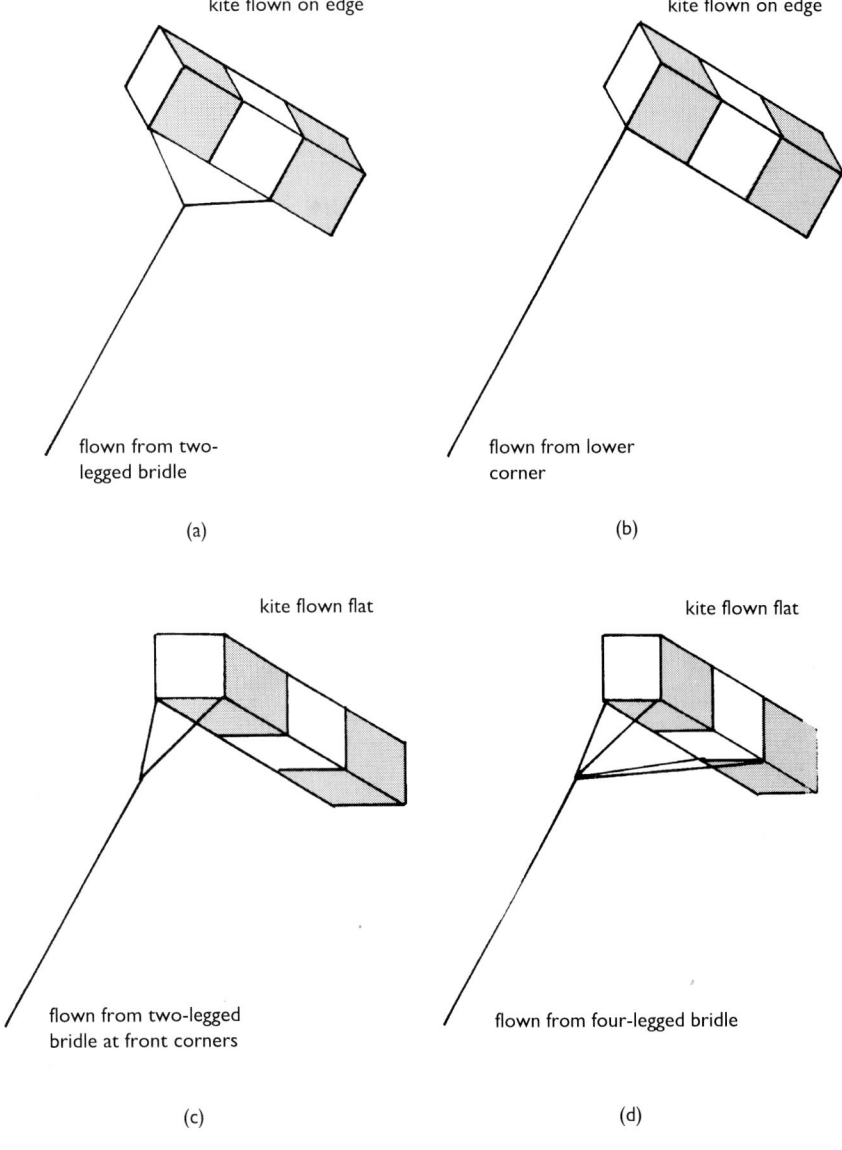

kite flown on edge

flown from two-legged bridle

(a)

kite flown on edge

flown from lower corner

(b)

kite flown flat

flown from two-legged bridle at front corners

(c)

kite flown flat

flown from four-legged bridle

(d)

METHOD

Note:
The structure of this kite is the same as the Rainbow kite, shown on pages 35–7.

I   Cut a cardboard template 400 × 400 mm to help with the marking out and to ensure that the kite is square. With the help of the template mark out two strips of nylon, 1610 mm long; this includes a 20 mm allowance for a joint. Mark lines across the cloth every 400 mm. Mark allowances down the sides as shown in Figure 10 overleaf.

2   Sew the two free ends of each of the strips together. Turn the completed cell inside-out so that the join is on the inside. Cut the longerons to size, and affix the plastic joints using one of the methods described on page 31. The longerons now need to be fitted into the cells. Generally, longerons would be fitted in pockets, but for a quick and simple kite, they can be

fixed in place with staples from a normal staple gun. Other kites in this book will show how more sophisticated pockets and fittings can be made.

3   To erect the kite, push the cross-spars into their plastic joints and tie them together with a length of line at the point at which they cross.

FLYING A SIMPLE BOX KITE

A box kite of polythene or cloth can be flown flat or from an edge (Figure 9a–d, previous page). To fly the kite flat, make a simple bridle by tying the ends of a two-metre length of flying line to the front ends of the two lower longerons before forming a loop in the centre, to which the flying line can be attached. With a two-legged bridle like this, the kite will adjust itself to the wind conditions and give a relatively gentle pull. The kite can also be flown flat from a four-

legged bridle. To fly the kite on edge, attach the flying line directly to the front lower corner of the kite; or use a two-legged bridle as shown.

A simple box kite will fly at a higher angle and give a greater pull when it is flown on edge, as a greater lifting surface is presented to the wind. However, the stability is reduced, because vertical panels give the greatest degree of stability. It is important to understand this principle, because it governs the performance of the kite in various wind conditions and also enables the flier to fly a kite in a greater range of wind speeds.

Flying a box kite on edge or as a rhombus (as opposed to a flat square) changes the aspect ratio of the kite: that is, the ratio of width to length. When flown as a rhombus, the aspect ratio is higher than when flown as a square and there is more lift, but the price to pay is a reduction in stability. Other kites of this type may be made, using the same method, by making the horizontal sides longer than the vertical sides.

RAINBOW BOX KITE

This is another simple box kite, and illustrates one of the ways in which ripstop nylon can be used to produce interesting visual effects. As ripstop cannot be easily painted on, joining pieces of material is a useful technique for creating patterns and designs.

The colours for a kite can be an important consideration and several factors will govern the final choice. If a kite is being designed to be admired on the ground or flown at relatively low altitudes then it is possible to use colours in almost any combinations. In the USA in particular, multi-coloured kites are frequently constructed with intricate geometrical designs. These look tremendous on or near the ground, but in the air the effect is lost and the excessive use of colour can be counter-productive in that a camouflage effect may result. For high-flying kites, the careful use of a few contrasting colours will often give a better visual impression.

Rainbow kite

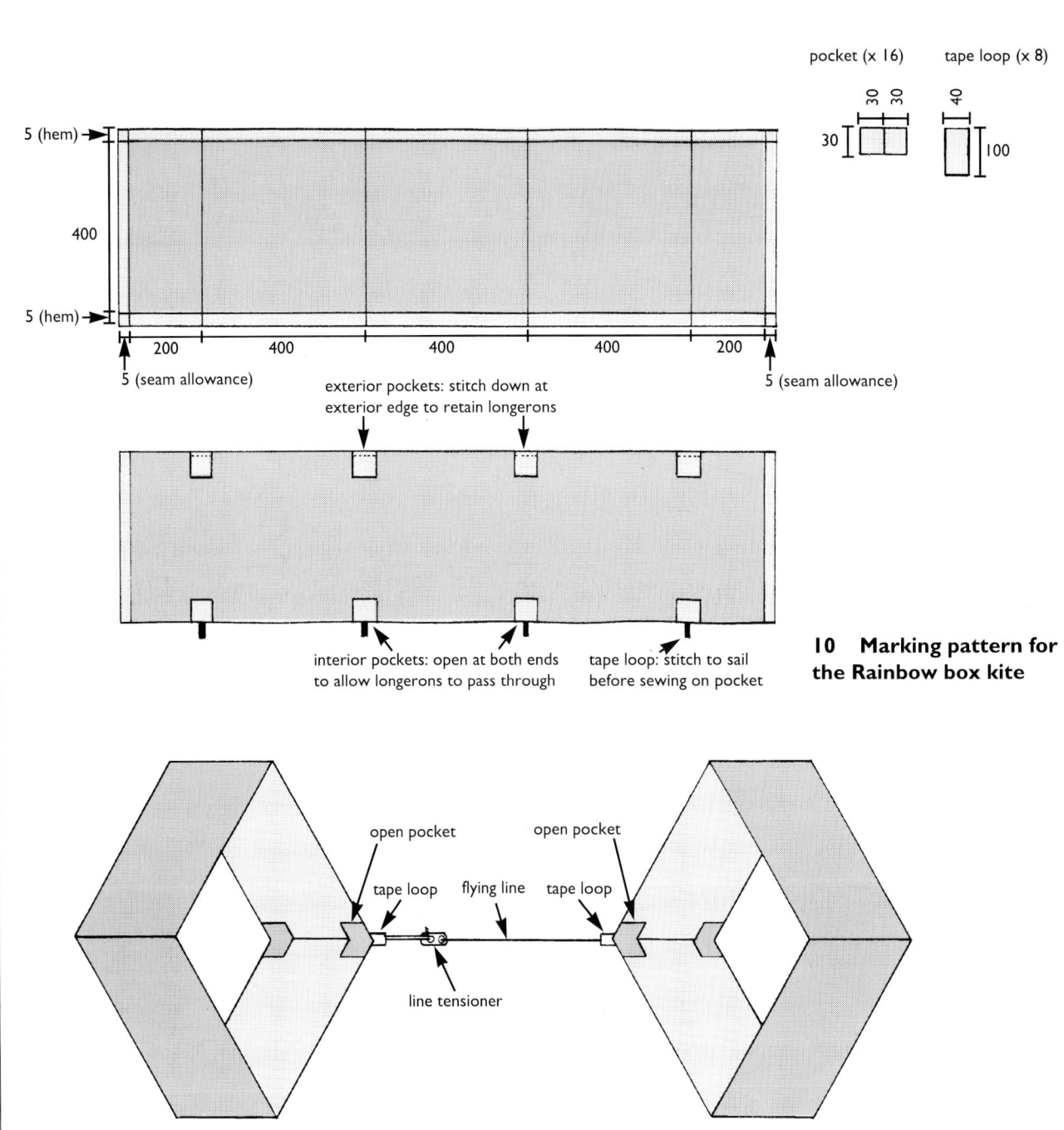

pocket (x 16)   tape loop (x 8)

5 (hem)
400
5 (hem)
5 (seam allowance)   200   400   400   400   200   5 (seam allowance)

exterior pockets: stitch down at exterior edge to retain longerons

interior pockets: open at both ends to allow longerons to pass through

tape loop: stitch to sail before sewing on pocket

10   Marking pattern for the Rainbow box kite

open pocket   open pocket
tape loop   flying line   tape loop
line tensioner
front cell   rear cell

This kite is braced by internal bracers held in position by joints made of plastic tubing as described in Figure 6 on page 31. It can be flown as a rectangle with a square section by using bracers of the same length, or as a rhombus by using asymmetric spars. The angle of the rhombus can be varied, but the dimensions of the spars given here will produce a 30° rhombus. The bracing spars are slightly longer than the calculated lengths to give tension to keep the panels taut.

11   Use of a cord-and-line tensioner to maintain the integrity of the cells: join all four internal corners of the front and rear cells to hold them together and maintain the overall shape of the kite

A box kite can have each cell made either from several panels or from a single piece of material with one join, either in the centre of a panel or at a corner. In this kite each of the cells will be made from a single piece of material, with the join which completes the cell located at the centre of a side, rather than at a corner.

MATERIALS

○ Fabric: ripstop nylon 2 x 1 m
○ Dacron tape (optional)
○ Longerons: hardwood dowel, four pieces 6 x 1200 mm
○ Diagonal spars for square: hardwood dowel, eight pieces 6 x 570 mm
○ Diagonal spars for 30° rhombus: hardwood dowel, four pieces 6 x 720 mm; four pieces 6 x 420 mm
○ Joints: fuel line (or other thermoplastic tubing), internal diameter 6 mm, length 500 mm
○ Line tensioners: four (optional)
○ Aluminum ring for bridling point

METHOD

1 Mark and cut out the fabric for the two cells of the kite (Figure 10). Mark clearly where the corners will fall and leave an allowance at each end for the seam which will complete the box sections. Cut out the two cells and sew the hems down the full length of the fabric.

2 Cut out the pockets from double-thickness ripstop or dacron tape, and stitch them to the sails as shown. The pockets which will be at the outer edges need to be stitched down the sides and across the ends, while those on the inner edges are only stitched down the sides so that the longerons can pass through them.

3 Sew tape loops 10 x 100 mm from four thicknesses of ripstop to join the two cells, and stitch them on to the inner edges so that they will be on the horizontal surface when the kite is assembled. Joining the cells as shown in Figure 11 enables more tension to be applied and prevents the cells falling off the longerons. Alternatively, you could use staples.

4 Assemble the kite with two sets of bracers, located in plastic joints as described on page 31, with each set 5 cm from the front and rear edges of each cell. Burn a small hole through the fabric at the bridling points using a hot soldering iron, and pass the bridle line through the holes. Tie the bridle line securely to the longerons (Figure 12). Form a loop at the towing point and fix an aluminium ring using a lark's-head hitch knot (see page 27).

5 This kite can be flown from a single corner, or from a two-legged bridle, if made as a square form (see Figure 9 on page 33, and page 34 for flying information). If in the form of a rhombus, use a two-legged bridle between a corner and a point on the same longeron just in front of the rear cell. The kite should be flown from line with a breaking strain of 35 kg (70 lb).

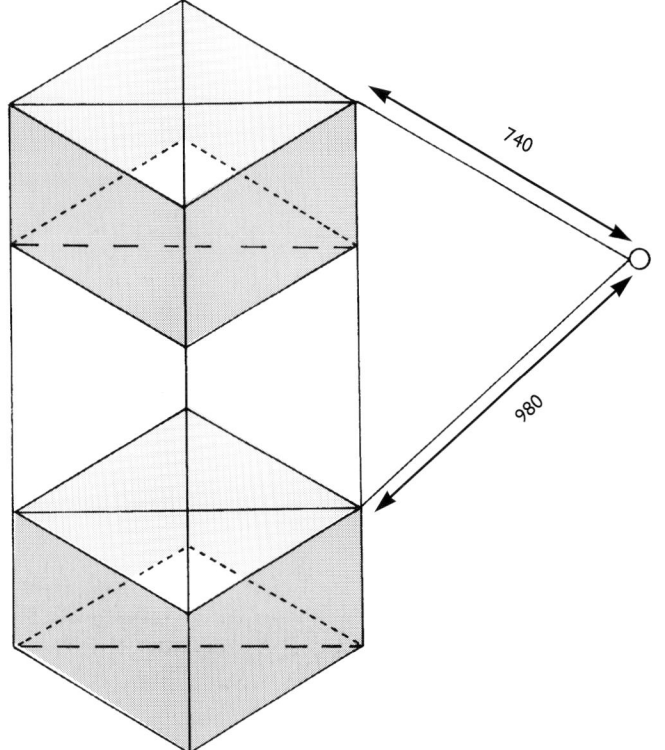

12 **Bridling points for the Rainbow box kite**

DICE BOX KITE

In the two-celled box kite, the separation of two cells by a space gives additional lateral stability, but the single-celled kite is lighter and more buoyant and is therefore a useful kite to fly in lighter winds.

The single cell presents a useful surface which can be used for a number of design exercises. The use of a dice or domino motif illustrates the use of appliqué to create an attractive design. Edge-binding (sewing a strip of material over the edge) was used to provide a strong edge and to create a sharp distinction between the sides. This is quite a time-consuming technique, but can be very effective and also saves the need for hemming to protect an exposed edge. In a kite such as this, any design could be used, with any combination of colours.

Dice kite

MATERIALS

○ Ripstop nylon: main colour 3·5 x 1 m; contrasting colour (dice motif) 1 x 0·5 m (or as required)
○ Longerons: hardwood dowel or fibreglass, four pieces 6 x 850 mm
○ Cross-spars: hardwood dowel, six pieces 6 x 1080 mm
○ Joints: fuel line (or other thermoplastic tubing), internal diameter 6 mm, length 500 mm
○ PVA adhesive
○ Plastic beads x 8
○ Arrow nocks x 8
○ Elastic bands x 6
○ Aluminium ring for bridling point

METHOD

1 Mark out the kite as shown in Figure 13, and cut out the four cells, with the seam allowances, as a single length of material. To edge-bind the kite, cut out the contrasting colour in strips 120 mm wide; fold the strips in half and iron with a cool iron so that the centre is clearly marked. Lightly glue the inside of the binding strip and wedge the edge of the material cut out for the cell in it. Press down firmly, making sure that the edge-binding is in the correct position, and then stitch down. Add the next strip in the same way.

2 Next, cut out the design you wish to apply. Lightly glue this in position on the side of the material which will become the outer surface and sew down. If a dark material is used for the appliqué, the material underneath should not show through. If a lighter material is used, it may be necessary to cut away the original material from beneath the newly applied piece. This technique is called cut-away appliqué.

Appliqué is not too difficult, but it is best to appliqué small pieces of material when you are first using the technique. If you are drawing up your own design, don't forget to take account of where the pockets will be, and try to keep your design away from them. After completing the decoration, sew down the hems before sewing the loops and pockets to the inside.

3 Mark out where the junctions between the sides of the cell will be, and, if you wish to separate them visually (as in the example shown), cut a piece of contrasting colour 60 mm wide and affix it on the line marking the boundary between the sides.

4 Using ripstop four layers thick, make eight tape loops 10 x 100 mm. Six of these can be sewn down on to the inside of the kite at the boundaries between the sides (Figure 14, overleaf). The last two cannot be affixed until the box section has been completed by sewing together the two inner edges.

5 Mark and cut out the pockets as shown. Three sets of pockets can be stitched into position, lightly held in position with adhesive if necessary (Figure 15, overleaf). Complete the cell by joining the two seam allowances. The neatest way to achieve this is to fold the

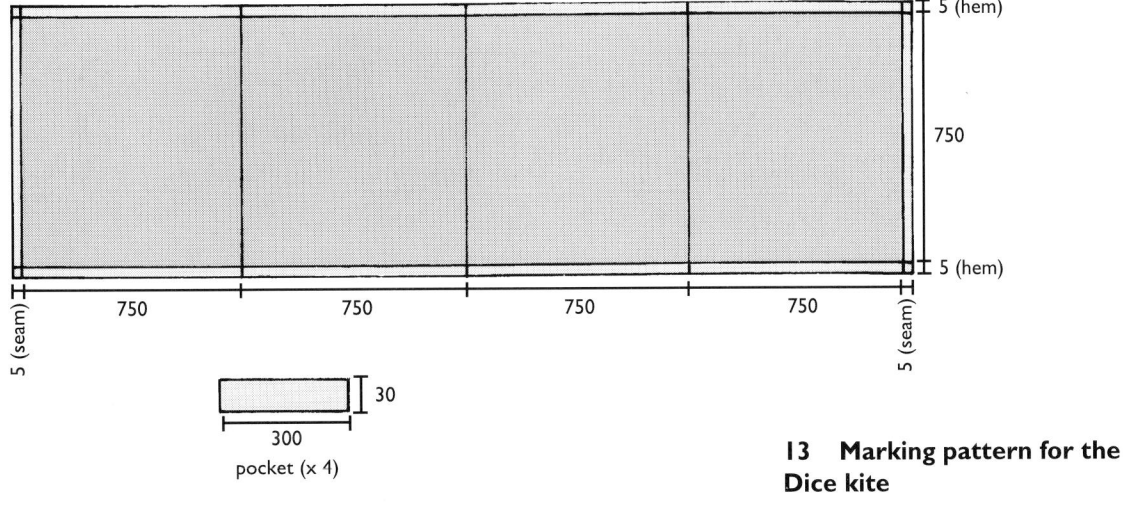

13 **Marking pattern for the Dice kite**

kite in half so that the outer surfaces touch, then glue the two seam allowances together before sewing with a double row of stitches for strength.

6 With the kite inside-out, the last piece of contrasting material at the cell boundary can be stitched into place, followed by the last two tape loops and finally the pockets.

7 Cut a short piece of line for each tape loop, thread it through the loop and affix a small plastic bead with 20 mm of line between loop and bead. The plastic beads will fit into an arrow nock fixed to the end of the longeron. Measure how long your longerons need to be to fit tightly into the loops when the arrow nocks are fitted, and cut them to size. The longerons may need to be slightly shorter or longer than the 850 mm stated, depending on the size of the line used, the size of the bead and the type of arrow nock. It is possible to use a notch cut into the end of the longeron instead of an arrow nock, but, when narrow dowel is used, it is difficult to make a suitable notch and the wood tends to split.

8 Push the longerons into the pockets through the plastic joints. Each spar has three joints, one at each end and one in the centre. Glue the arrow nocks to the ends of the longerons and stretch the beads over them. Cut the diagonal spars slightly longer than you think they should be to achieve a good tension. Use a strong elastic band to join them together at the centre point, and fit them into the joints to brace the kite. Trim the ends of the longerons if necessary so that a good, tight fit is obtained.

9 This kite can be flown flat, on edge or from a corner (see Figure 9 on page 33), but will pull harder if flown on edge. The kite is very light for its sail area, and is suitable for flying in a light wind from 50 kg (100 lb) breaking-strain line. To fly in stronger winds, the hardwood longerons may be replaced with fibreglass or thicker dowel.

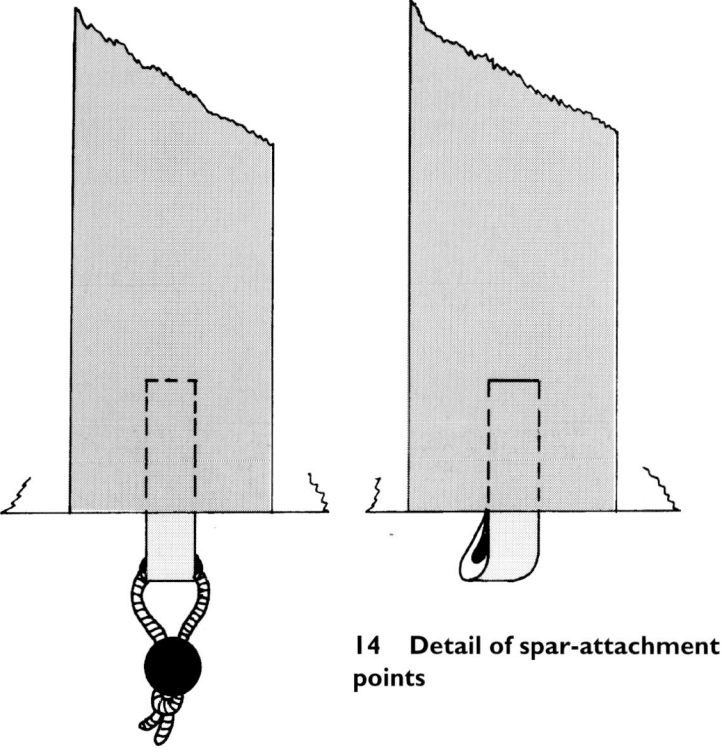

14 Detail of spar-attachment points

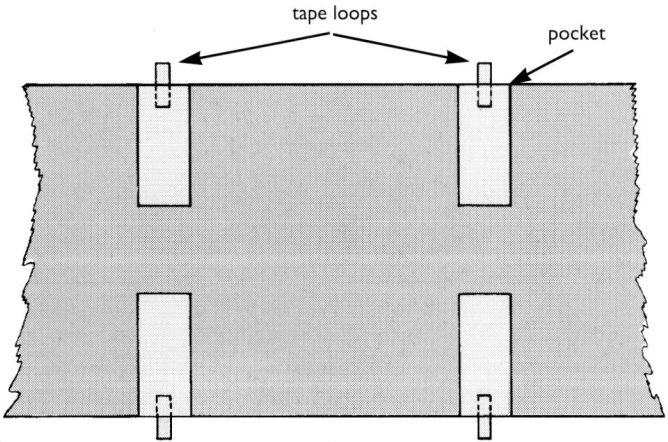

tape loops

pocket

15 Arrangement of loops and pockets

SINGLE-CELLED TETRAHEDRON
MADE FROM BAMBOO AND PLASTIC SHEETING

Some of Alexander Bell's tetrahedral kites were giant structures with thousands of cells, and a multi-celled example is shown here. The basic principles can be easily followed to produce simple tetrahedral structures, the instructions for which are given overleaf. These kites have considerable strength by virtue of the bracing inherent to the design, and are good heavy-weather kites. A simple tetrahedral kite can be quickly fabricated from pre-cut small bamboo canes available from garden centres. The frame can be assembled by tying the joints with string and then soaking the string with PVA adhesive to give a strong finish.

Bell's tetrahedral kite

MATERIALS

○ Plastic sheet for sails: 1·5 m x 600 mm
○ 6 x bamboo strips, approx. 4 mm diameter x 60 mm (or 6 mm dowel)
○ Elastic bands x 6
○ Thin string: approx. 5 m
○ PVA adhesive
○ Clear adhesive tape (such as Sellotape)
○ Aluminium ring for bridling point

METHOD

The cell can be made to any size up to approx. 1m across, but the kite described here is based upon an equilateral triangle with a side 500 mm long and framing sticks 600 mm long.

1 Take the six pieces of bamboo and form them into the shape of a tetrahedron, creating temporary joints using elastic bands at the corners. Allow an overlap of approx. 10 mm between the sticks at each corner. Soak the string in water and cut into six equal lengths. Starting at one corner, remove the elastic band and tie the string tightly around the sticks, finishing with a secure knot. Repeat this process at each of the corners until all the temporary joints have been replaced.

2 As the string dries it will contract, pulling the sticks closer together to form a very tight joint. When the string is completely dry, soak the joints with PVA adhesive and allow to dry.

3 Make a cardboard template of an equilateral triangle with a side length of 500 mm, cutting off the corners as shown, or use the kite frame as a template. In this case, fold your sail material in half and draw a line along the fold. Lay the frame on the fold and draw around it to mark the sails. Mark an allowance of 50 mm for folding over

and cut off the corners (Figure 16c). Stretch the plastic over two adjacent sides and fold the allowances over the frame. Stick down the plastic using clear adhesive tape.

4 The kite flies inverted. A line may be attached directly to the kite at a point one-third of the distance along the common side, or else flown from a two-legged bridle formed from a one-metre length of line tied to the ends of a common side. Find the towing point in the field to suit the wind speed. The kite should be flown from line with a breaking strain of 50 kg (100 lb).

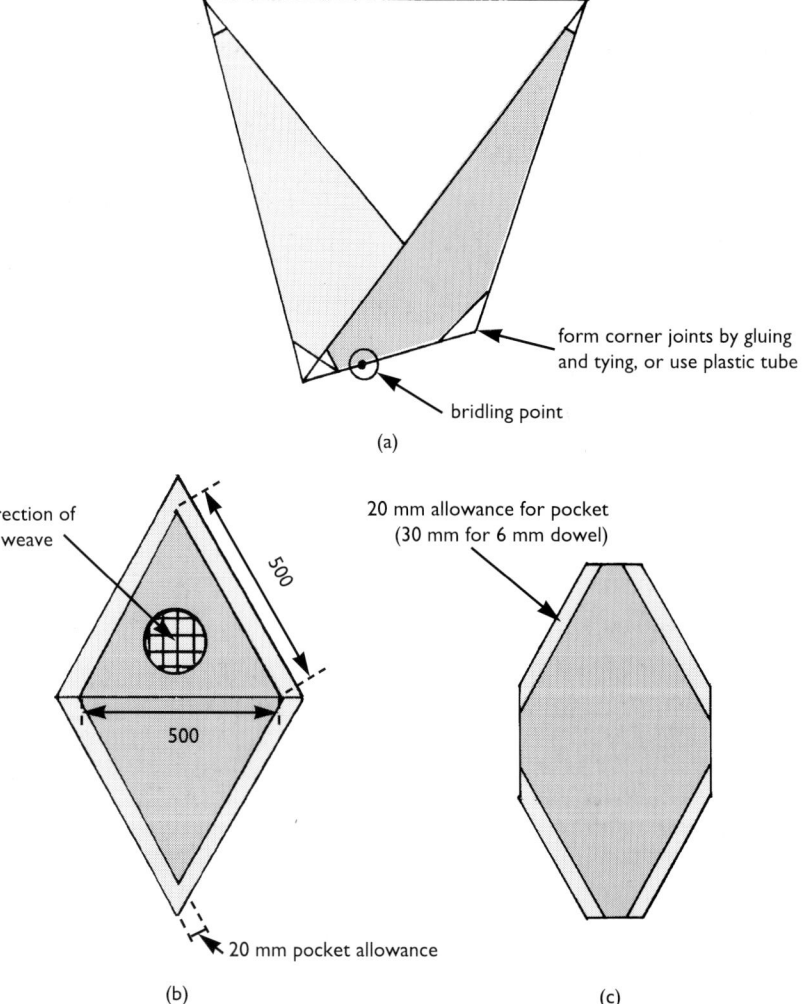

form corner joints by gluing and tying, or use plastic tube

bridling point

(a)

direction of weave

500

500

20 mm pocket allowance

20 mm allowance for pocket (30 mm for 6 mm dowel)

(b)

(c)

16   Single-celled tetrahedron: (a) basic structure showing bridling point (b) marking pattern for cell (c) completed panel

SINGLE-CELLED TETRAHEDRON
MADE FROM RIPSTOP NYLON

A more refined version of the tetrahedron can be made from ripstop nylon and fibreglass or dowel.

1 As a first step it is necessary to create a more suitable way of joining the sticks together at the corners. The easiest method is to cut three short lengths of thermoplastic tubing, flatten one end of each tube longitudinally and then to join the tubes together in the flattened region.

2 To create the joints, cut lengths of tubing 50 mm long, flatten them, and then make a small hole through the flattened region with a soldering iron or a drill. Repeat this process with three lengths of tube, which are then joined together with a small nut and bolt, a rivet or even wire to form a three-way joint.

3 Make a template to cut the sails as shown in Figure 16(b) and sew pockets down the sides. The spars are passed through the pockets and are then pushed into the corner joints. This kite may be flown from line with a breaking strain of about 50 kg (100 lb).

Single-celled tetrahedron

HARGRAVE BOX KITE

Hargrave's work with kite design seems to have ended with the development of the perfected cellular kite, but the importance of this should not be forgotten, as it formed the basis of the early aeroplane. A full-sized Hargrave kite is a formidable performer, but even the half-sized form described here gives remarkable lift in a fresh wind.

MATERIALS

○ Ripstop nylon or other fabric: 3·5 x 1 m
○ Wing longerons: hardwood dowel, sixteen pieces 6 x 400 mm
○ Bracers: hardwood dowel, eight pieces 6 x 750 mm
○ Central longerons: 9 mm fibreglass, two pieces 9 x 1200 mm
○ Plastic tube for joints: internal diameter 6 mm, length 480 mm
○ Line tensioners x 2 (optional)
○ Dacron tape (optional)
○ PVC insulating tape
○ Elastic band or 'O' ring
○ Aluminium ring for bridling point

Hargrave kite

METHOD

The original Hargrave kite had no pockets; the longerons had notches near the tips and the fabric of the cells was tied into these. Sufficient tension was developed to hold the whole structure in place. On smaller versions, the lighter materials do not have sufficient strength to enable the same degree of tension to be placed on them. In this half-sized version, pockets were constructed to accommodate the longerons. The general construction of the kite is shown in Figures 17 and 18.

The advantage of using 6 mm dowel for the shorter longerons and for the cross-bracers is that it reduces the weight of the finished kite and enables simple plastic joints to be used, rather than having to fashion purpose-built ones.

1 Cut out the panels and pockets (Figure 19, overleaf) and sew down the hems where appropriate. Make the pockets which will hold the fibreglass longerons from double-thickness nylon, or dacron tape, to reinforce the ends. The front and rear cells are made from two longer upper/lower surfaces joined to two smaller side panels. Hem the panels and sew on the small pockets as shown. Form the pockets at the four corners as shown on page 36.

2 Cut out a hole at the central area of each of the corner pockets, so that a plastic joint can be fitted through before the pocket is stitched down. Next, sew the shorter (400 mm) dowel lengths into their pockets. It is a good idea to put a small bevel on the ends, using a pencil sharpener and sandpaper, so that they may be more easily stitched down. The arrangement of the plastic joints is shown in Figure 20 (overleaf).

3 On the front cell, stitch across the pockets for the fibreglass longerons at the front; it is a good idea to reinforce this area with dacron tape if available. Leave the rear edge open. On the rear cell,

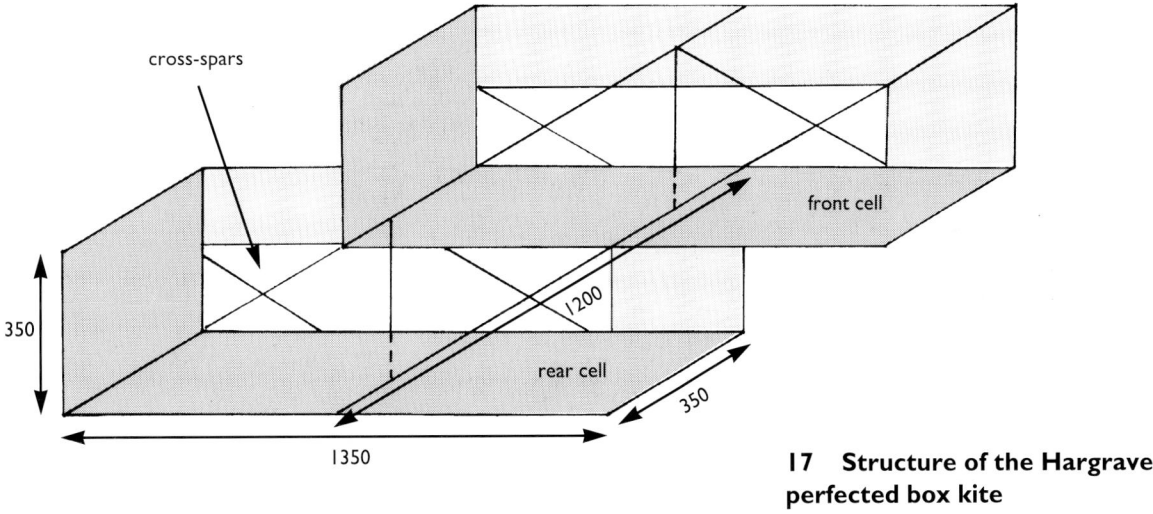

cross-spars

front cell

350

1200

rear cell

350

1350

17 Structure of the Hargrave perfected box kite

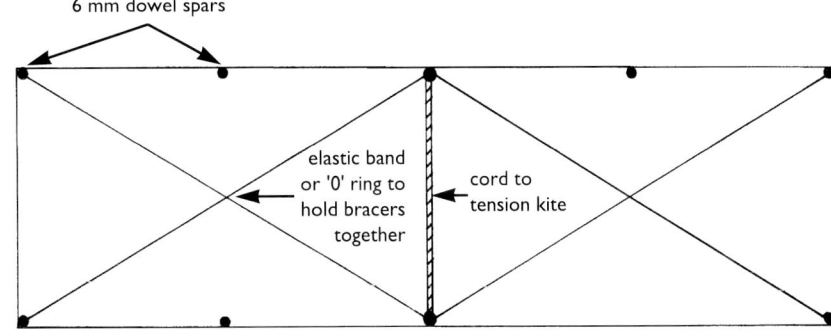

6 mm dowel spars

elastic band or '0' ring to hold bracers together

cord to tension kite

18 Side elevation showing position of bracers and tensioning cord

follow the same method, but sew down the rear edge. Cut the fibreglass rod to size using a small hacksaw: do this out-of-doors or wear a dust mask. Cover the ends of the fibreglass with PVC insulating tape or a rubber end-cap to prevent the fibreglass cutting the fabric.

4   Slot the fibreglass rods into their pockets with two plastic joints at the centre of the upper and lower surfaces of the front and rear cells. Take the cross-bracers and form them into pairs held together by an elastic band or 'O' ring at the central point. Fit the ends of the cross-bracers into the plastic joints and the kite will assume its shape.

5   Cut two lengths of flying line about a metre long and tie them to the fibreglass rod at the centre of each cell, between the plastic joints. A line tensioner may be used to adjust the pressure and get the correct tension on the sails. The sails should be very taut.

6   Finally, use a small soldering iron to put a small hole in the lower surface of the front cell below the fibreglass rod and 20 cm from the front edge. Slot a one-metre length of flying line through and tie securely to the fibreglass rod at one end, and tie the aluminium ring at the other as an attachment point for the flying line.

7   Fly the kite in moderate to fresh winds from 70 kg (150 lb) breaking-strain line.

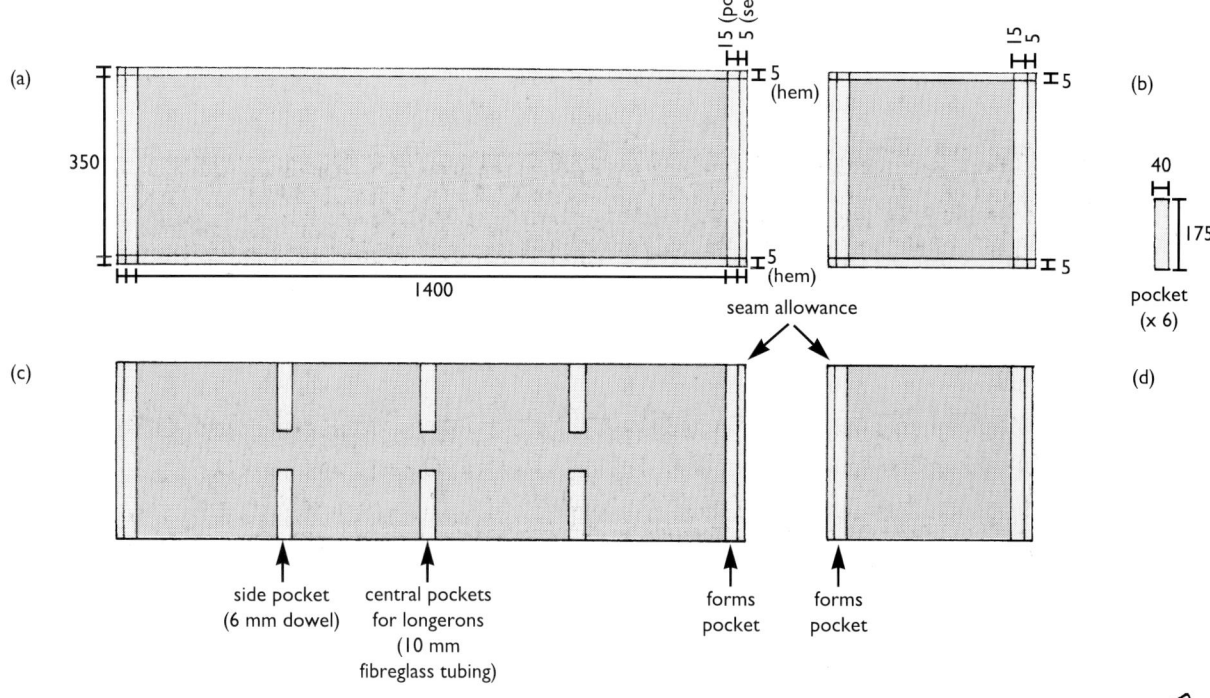

19   Marking pattern:
(a) upper/lower wing sections x 4
(b) side panels x 4 (c) completed wing sections (d) completed side panels

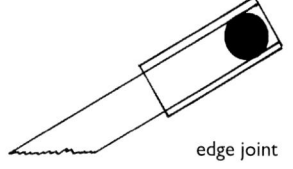

edge joint

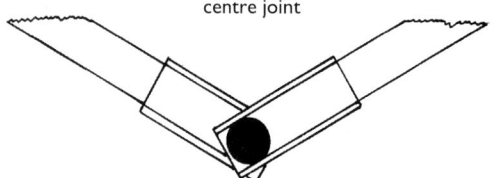

centre joint

20   Joints on the Hargrave perfected kite

SAUL'S NAVAL BARRAGE KITE

Saul's naval barrage kite is a development of the Hargrave perfected box kite, in which additional box sections have been added to the front wing, with a panel down the centre of the kite, to give increased directional stability. The barrage kite is aesthetically pleasing, stable in flight, and can be constructed so that it may be flown with different combinations of longerons and bracers in a variety of wind conditions from light to strong.

The version described here is designed around a panel size of 350 mm, and a lightweight version can be made using 6 mm hardwood dowel for both spars and bracers, although it is better to use 6 mm fibreglass for the longerons as this gives a much stronger kite.

Saul's naval barrage kite

Some books suggest that, in small versions of this kite, a single, cent-rally placed set of spars can be used to reduce weight. With this method of construction, however, it is difficult to achieve even tensioning. The use of double sets of spars to the front and rear of each cell, and string-tensioning lines between the upper and lower panels (as in the Hargrave kite) can be used to produce a better and more even tension in the cells.

Another modification worth trying is to reduce the length of the longerons so that the space between the front and rear wings is equal to the width of the cells, rather than twice the width of the cells as in the original. This gives a more compact kite with a slightly reduced weight. In theory, reducing the space between the front and rear cells should reduce stability,

but I have not found this to be a problem on the smaller versions.

MATERIALS

○ **Ripstop nylon or other fabric: 5 x 1 m**
○ **Longerons: fibreglass rod or tube, six pieces 6 x 1855 mm**
○ **Longerons for edges of front wing: 6 mm hardwood dowel, four pieces 6 x 370 mm**
○ **Cell bracers: hardwood dowel, twelve pieces 6 x 500 mm**
○ **Joints: thermoplastic tubing, internal diameter 6 mm, length 1200 mm**
○ **Cardboard**
○ **Plastic beads x 14**
○ **Elastic bands x 6**
○ **Arrow nocks: 14 pieces, internal diameter 6 mm**
○ **Aluminium ring for bridling point**

METHOD

1 Make a cardboard template 350 x 350 mm and use it to mark out the panels (Figures 21 and 22), adding hem and other allowances as appropriate. Cut the panels to size and sew hems along the front and rear edges of each panel.

2 Mark and cut out the material which will be used for the pockets which are not formed at the corners of the box sections; these are found at the centre of the front panels and 350 mm to each side of it, and in the centre of the rear box section.

3 At the same time, cut out the rectangle of material which will fit into the centre of the kite, starting in the front wing and extending rearwards. In order to form a pocket on each of the long sides of this panel, it is necessary to sew on additional strips of material (Figure 23).

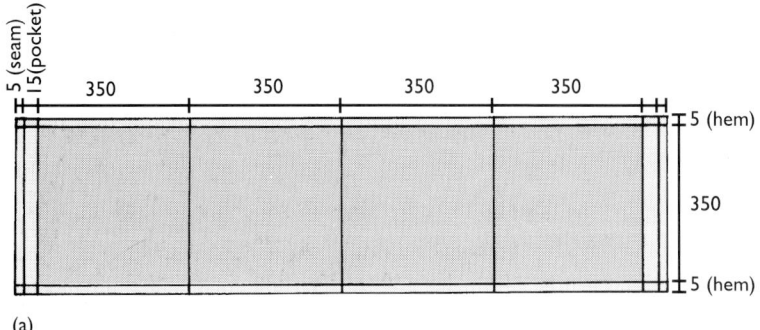
(a)

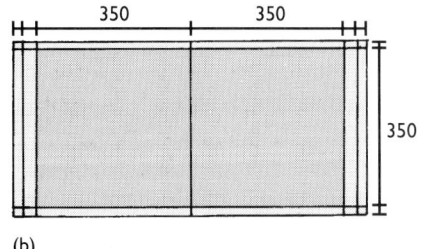
(b)

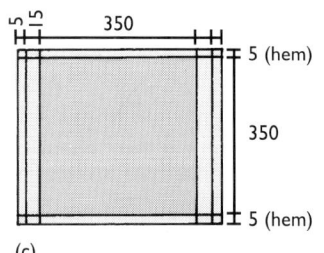
(c)

21 Marking pattern: (a) front wing: upper/lower surface x 2 (b) rear wing: upper/lower surface x 2 (c) side panels x 4

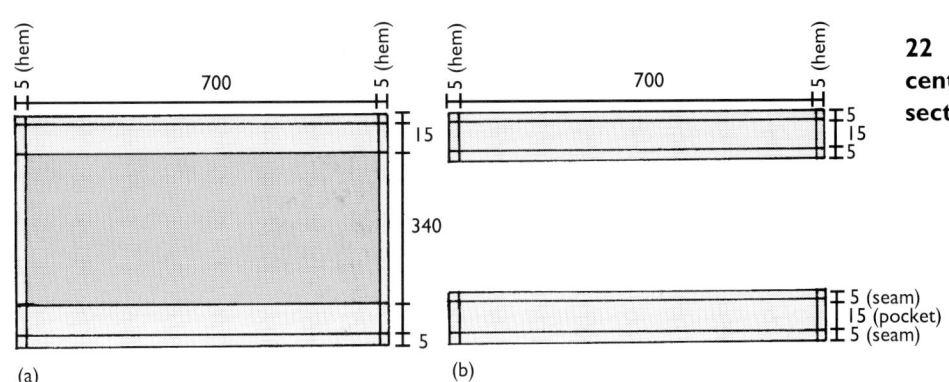

22   Marking pattern: (a) front centre panel x 1 (b) pocket sections x 2

23   Assembly: (a) front centre section (b) front centre section between wings

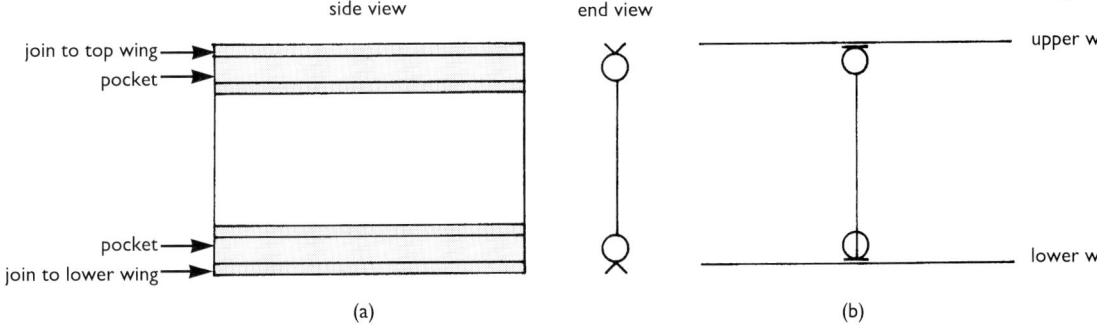

4   To assemble the front wing, first stitch the centre panel to the inside surfaces of both the upper and lower front-wing sections. To complete the box, sew the side panels on to the upper and lower panels by putting the outer surfaces together, sewing across the seam line and corner line and opening up the joint, which then encloses a pocket. The pockets can be on the inside or outside of the box. The rear wing is slightly simpler and is also formed by sewing the side panels to the inside of the upper and lower wing sections.

5   The pockets may be completed by sewing across the outer edges if you wish to use a single central set of bracers, but it is better to use open pockets, employing the notch-and-bead method to locate the longerons (see page 24). If

you wish to use a single set of bracers, small holes to accommodate the plastic joints which locate the bracers will need to be made carefully in the centre of the pockets.

6   The wing bracers are located using joints made from 50 mm pieces of plastic tube (see page 31); 24 of these will be required. The bracers are fitted in pairs. Take a pair of bracers and join them at the centre point with a strong elastic band. To fit each pair, simply open them out to form a cross, and push into the plastic joints. To produce additional rigidity, tie central bracing cords in the middle of the cells between the upper and lower surfaces (see Figure 18 on page 45). The completed kite is shown in Figure 24 (overleaf).

7   This kite traditionally uses a five-legged bridle. A line is taken from the front of the forward longerons to a point one-and-a-quarter times the length of the longerons, below the central longeron. The lines can be attached by sewing tapes to the lower front edge, or by using a soldering iron to burn small holes on each side of the longerons. Fix 154 cm of line with a ring attached to the central lower longeron. The other bridle lines can then be easily joined to this point. This system allows the kite to find its own flying angle, and, because of the multiple legs to the bridle, the load is evenly spread.

8   Fly the kite from 70 kg (150 lb) breaking-strain line in moderate to fresh winds.

24   Assembled barrage kite

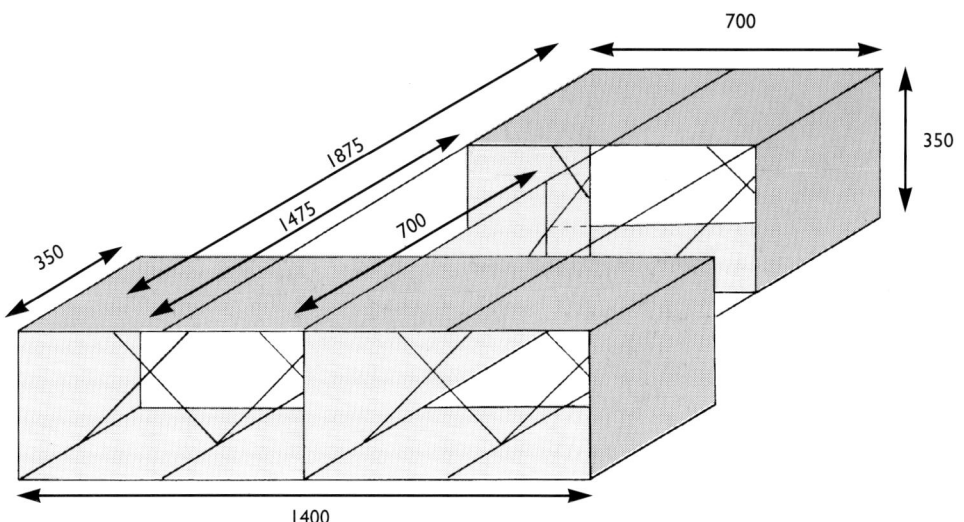

FOUR

WINGED BOX KITES

CONYNE BOX KITE

The Conyne kite (also known as the French Signal kite) is a compound triangular kite. It is relatively simple to make, is adaptable in size and is an excellent flier. It can, however, be a very unforgiving kite, and any lack of symmetry is punished by flying to one side. With a multi-legged bridle, this tendency may be corrected by adjustments, but in the Conyne, the two-legged bridle is attached to the central, lower longeron and this option is not available.

The wings must be stretched tightly by the cross-spars, to maintain the correct shape of the triangular box sections. It is possible to brace the Conyne with a single spar between the wing-tips, but with larger models it is better to use another spar to brace the rear box section tightly. The spars should fit very tightly across the kite, producing a slight bowing which will increase stability. To reduce weight, the shorter rear spar may be made of thinner wood than the front spar. It is possible to add a bow cord to give extra bowing, but this should not be necessary if the spar fits tightly enough across the wing.

Conyne kite

An important point concerns the weave of the fabric. When fabric is cut at an angle across the bias, it has a tendency to stretch, especially if it is in an area of the kite which is under stress. In a properly constructed Conyne, with a tightly fitting cross-spar, the wings are under stress, and it is therefore important to reduce stretching both during manufacture and flight.

The simplest way to make the wing is to cut it as a single piece of cloth, but if this is done there will inevitably be stretching along the edges cut across the bias, often made worse as the material is hemmed. When the kite is flown, further stretching may occur, leading to asymmetry and poor flight.

MATERIALS

○ Ripstop nylon or other fabric: 5 x 1 m
○ Longerons: hardwood dowel, three pieces 9 x 1300 mm
○ Spar: *light winds*: dowel, one piece 9 x 1300 mm
○ Spar: *fresh winds*: dowel, one piece 12 x 1300 mm
○ PVA adhesive
○ Dacron tape (optional)
○ Cardboard
○ Plastic beads x 8
○ Line tensioner (optional)
○ Aluminium ring for bridling point

METHOD

There are several variations on the basic design, in that the space between cells can be varied. As this one is intended for lighter winds, the central space between the cells is the same as that of the cells. For stronger winds the space between the cells can be increased to one-and-a-half or even twice the size of the cells, increasing stability but at the cost of greater weight. With most kites there is no absolute construction method, and the following is offered as one suggested approach.

1 The wings are each made in two pieces, to minimize stretching (Figure 25). Mark and cut as shown so that the weave of the material runs along the outer edges. Join the two sections together with a medium-sized stitch, using either a flat (lap) seam or a double seam (Figure 26).

2 Form a hem on the upper surface around the two outside edges of the wing. Fold the pocket and secure with adhesive before stitching down. Reinforce the point of the wing with a semi-circular patch of doubled ripstop or dacron tape.

3 Once the point has been reinforced, sew into place tape loops 10 x 100 mm made from four thicknesses of ripstop, and fit a plastic bead to the loops with a short length of flying line, as shown in Figure 14 on page 40. A short pocket may be fitted to the upper surface of the wings to hold the cross-spar in place, but on smaller kites this can be dispensed with to simplify construction.

4 The box sections need to be cut and marked accurately, and the best way to do this is to cut out a

400

40 (pocket)
5 (seam)

400   5 (seam)   5 (seam)   800

25   Marking pattern for wing x 2

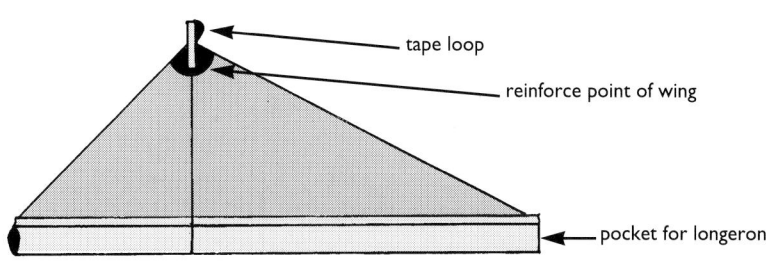

tape loop

reinforce point of wing

pocket for longeron

26   Completed wing x 2

square cardboard template 400 × 400 mm. Draw round the template to give two 400 mm squares, then mark in hem and seam allowances to give two upper panels and two lower panels (Figures 27 and 28). Stitch down the seam allowances as shown.

5 For the upper panel, there will be a hem down the sides and a seam allowance, while the lower panels will have material for a seam with the lower surface of the wing pocket. Join the upper panels to the wing sections (Figures 29 and 30). When the wings have been joined by the upper panels, turn the kite so that the under surface is facing up, and sew the lower panels in place.

6 Stitch along at the lower edge to form the bottom pocket. The longerons are located in their pockets either by stitching across the outer edges, or by using a tape-loop and plastic-bead system (see Figure 14 on page 40).

7 Erect the kite by means of a cross-spar between the two points of the wing, making sure that the wing is stretched tightly. For larger kites, a second cross-spar may be fitted across the kite just in front of the rear cells, and to do this tape loops will need to be sewn on to the wing level with the front edges of the rear cell. The lower edges of the triangular box sections should be tied to each other using the tape loops fitted to the lower internal corners of the triangular sections. Alternatively, the longerons could be stapled to the panels.

8 There are various positions for the bridle, but perhaps the best option is to tie a two-legged bridle to the lower longeron at the nose of the kite and just in front of the rear cell. Even a small Conyne gives a strong pull in a fresh wind, and line with a breaking strain of about 70 kg (150 lb) is recommended.

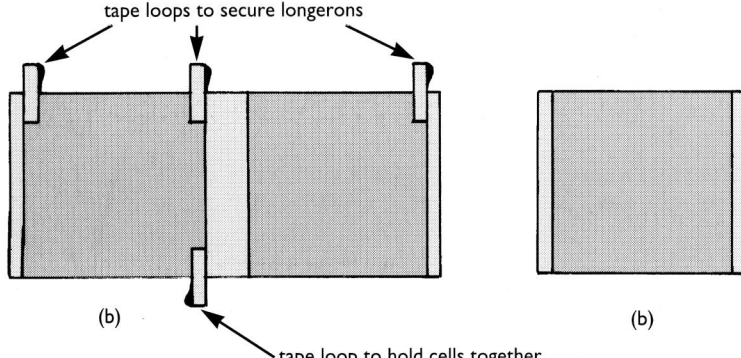

27 Lower panel x 2: (a) marking pattern (b) completed panel

28 Upper panel x 2: (a) marking pattern (b) completed panel

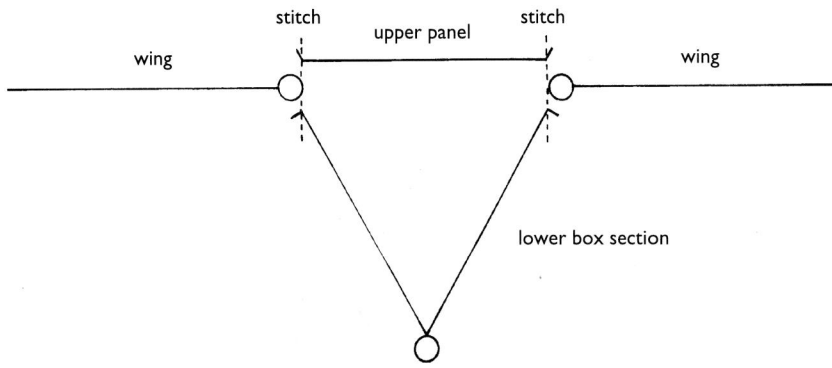

29 Assembly of the Conyne kite

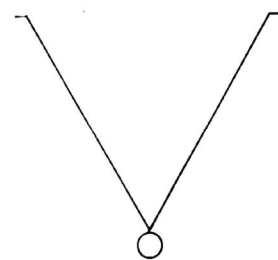

30 Completed lower panel

FRENCH RESCUE KITE

This is a very interesting kite and one which tends to be overlooked. It was apparently developed by the French Military as a means of carrying a line between ship and shore to facilitate rescue from shipwrecks.

The rescue kite has three triangular box sections as opposed to the two found in the Conyne kite. The wing is also a different shape, being in the form of an isosceles triangle, producing different flying characteristics. The Conyne is a fine flier and in a fresh wind can give a somewhat vicious pull, whereas a rescue kite gives a steadier and more controlled pull. The rescue kite also performs well in moderate winds and has been known to win altitude contests. It is an attractive kite with a very pleasing symmetry.

French rescue kite

MATERIALS

○ Ripstop nylon or other fabric:
6 x 1 m
○ Longerons: hardwood dowel,
three pieces 9 x 1600 mm
○ Spar: *light winds*: dowel, one
piece 9 x 2200 mm
○ Spar: *fresh winds*: dowel, one
piece 12 x 2200 mm
○ Dacron tape (optional)
○ Plastic beads x 8
○ Line tensioner (optional) x 2
○ Aluminium ring for bridling point

METHOD

This kite is built in the same way as
the Conyne and, once again, accur-
acy is critical.

1   Cut each wing in two pieces
(Figure 31), with the direction of
the grain running parallel to the
outer edges, then form the wing by
stitching the two halves together
(Figure 32). Stitch on the wing
pockets for the cross-spar, and
reinforce the wing-tip with a double
thickness of ripstop or dacron tape,
before sewing on a 10 x 100 mm
tape loop made from four thicknesses of ripstop. To this loop can
be fixed a loop made from a short
length of flying line and a plastic
bead, as described for the Conyne
(see page 53).

2   Mark and cut out the box
panels (Figures 33 and 34) and sew
hems down the outer edges. You
will need tape loops at the outer
edge of the pockets to accommodate the notch-and-bead system for
locating the longerons; or, if you
prefer, stitch across the ends of the
pockets to accommodate the
longerons. Tape loops can also be
sewn to the inside faces, so that
lines can be tied between the panels to maintain the shape of the kite
in flight. Alternatively, staples could
be used to hold the lower longeron
in position.

3   Sew down the bottom pocket
with a double row of stitches. This
kite is traditionally bridled with a
three-legged bridle (Figure 35): it is
therefore necessary to stitch a small
tape loop to the central points of
the lower panels, just above the
pocket formed for the lower
longeron. As an alternative, make
small holes on each side of the
panels using a soldering iron, to
allow the bridle to pass round the
lower longeron and be tied to it.

4   The kite is assembled in the
same way as the Conyne kite (see
page 54), with the upper panels
being sewn into place first, followed
by the lower ones. Cut the
longerons to size and locate them
in their pockets using your chosen
method. Join the lower cells with
lengths of line to keep them in
place: the use of a line tensioner on
each will allow easy adjustments.

5   The kite is very quickly erected
by inserting the horizontal spar into
the bead attachments at the ends
of the wings – it can literally be
assembled in seconds. It is best
flown with the bridle set fairly
square to the wind. Use a flying line
of 70 to 100 kg (150 to 200 lb)
breaking strain.

31   **Marking pattern for wing x 2**

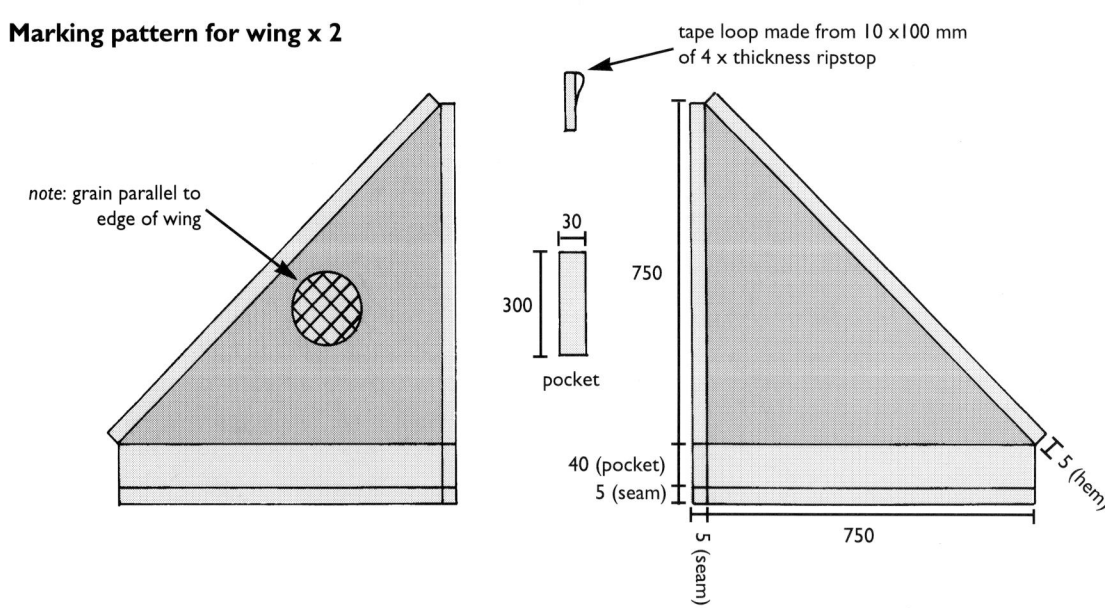

note: grain parallel to
edge of wing

tape loop made from 10 x100 mm
of 4 x thickness ripstop

30

300

pocket

750

750

40 (pocket)
5 (seam)

5 (seam)

5 (hem)

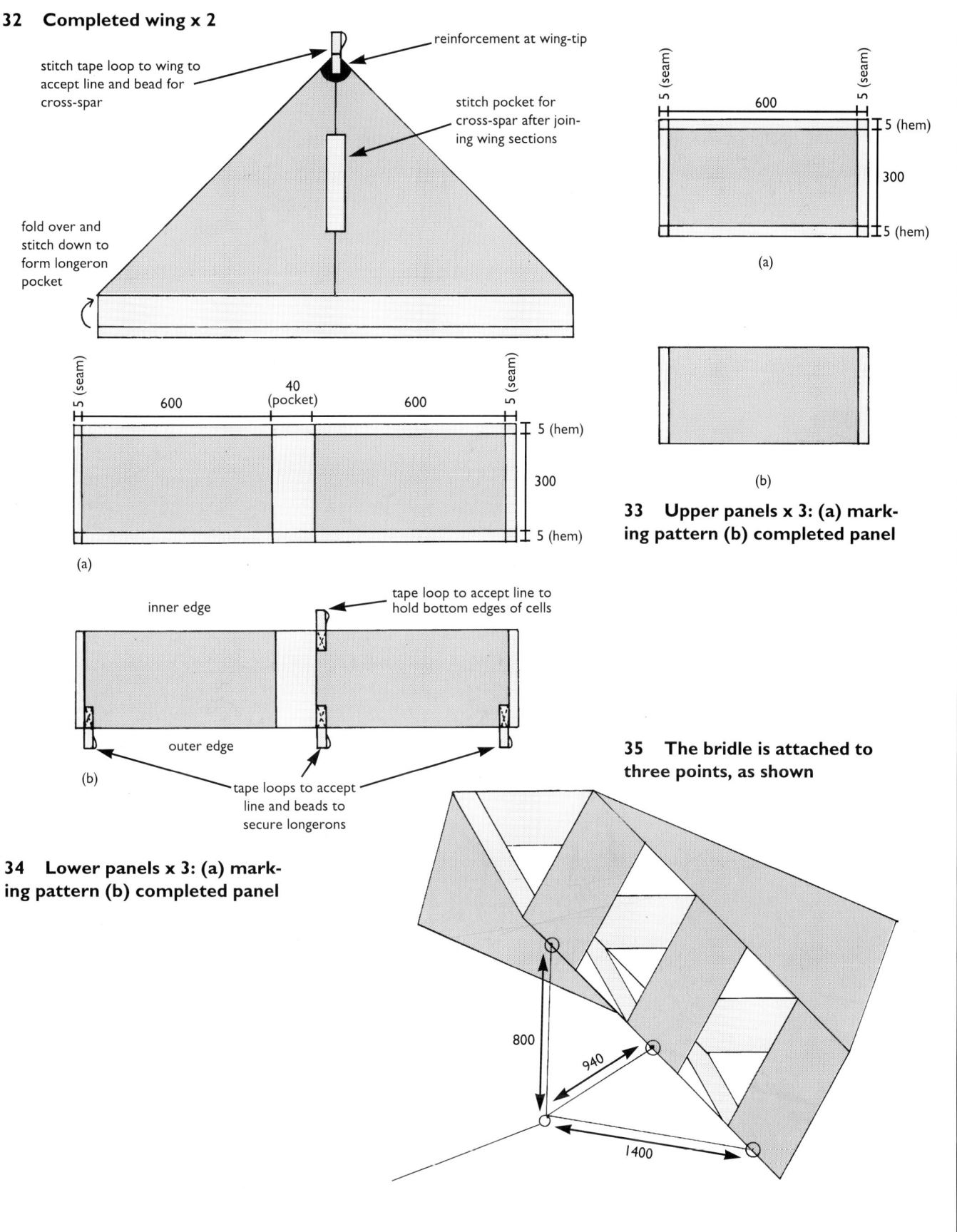

32   Completed wing x 2

stitch tape loop to wing to accept line and bead for cross-spar

reinforcement at wing-tip

stitch pocket for cross-spar after join-ing wing sections

fold over and stitch down to form longeron pocket

5 (seam)

600

40 (pocket)

600

5 (seam)

5 (hem)

300

5 (hem)

(a)

inner edge

tape loop to accept line to hold bottom edges of cells

outer edge

(b)

tape loops to accept line and beads to secure longerons

34   Lower panels x 3: (a) mark-ing pattern (b) completed panel

5 (seam)

5 (seam)

600

5 (hem)

300

5 (hem)

(a)

(b)

33   Upper panels x 3: (a) mark-ing pattern (b) completed panel

35   The bridle is attached to three points, as shown

800

940

1400

TRIPLE-STACK DELTA CONYNE

This is an interesting design, originating with Alan Davies of the Northern Kite Group and modified by Harry Peart of the North-east Kite-fliers. Three delta wings of increasing size are linked by box sections. The very lowest box section (which contains the bridling points) is triangular, the upper two are rectangular. There is no reason why more sections could not be added to give an even greater stack.

MATERIALS

○ Fabric: ripstop nylon, 4 x 1 m
○ Spars in outer pockets: hardwood dowel or fibreglass tube: upper wing, two pieces 6 x 1000 mm; middle wing, two pieces 6 x 750 mm; lower wing, two pieces 6 x 602 mm
○ Longerons: hardwood dowel, seven pieces 6 x 460 mm
○ Spreader bars: hardwood dowel (or 5–6 mm fibreglass tube): upper wing, 9 x 620 mm (approx.); middle wing, 9 x 420 mm (approx.); lower wing, 9 x 256 mm (approx.)
○ Plastic beads x 14
○ Small aluminium rings x 7
○ Aluminium ring for bridling point

Triple-stack Delta Conyne

58

METHOD

The size of the wings varies, but the pattern of construction is the same.

I   Mark and cut out the wings with the allowances for pockets and hems (Figures 36 and 37). Ensure that the grain of the fabric is parallel with the outer edge of the wing to avoid stretching. Sew the hem which runs along the trailing (rear) edge of the wing.

2   The outer pocket, which runs along the outer edge of each wing, houses a 6 mm hardwood dowel. Form the pocket by folding over the pocket allowance and stitching it down parallel to the edge of the wing. Sew across the top of the pocket.

3   The pocket which houses the longeron is formed by folding over the allowance, but leave the ends of the pocket open. Measure 150 mm from the front, down this pocket, and draw a line at 90°

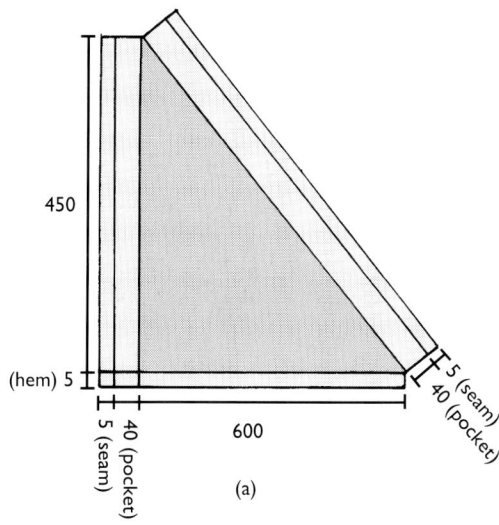

(a)

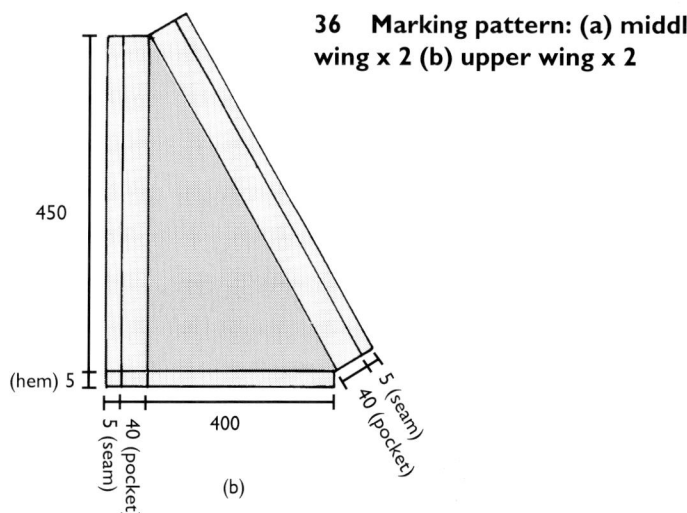

36   Marking pattern: (a) middle wing x 2 (b) upper wing x 2

(b)

37   Marking pattern and construction of lower wing x 2

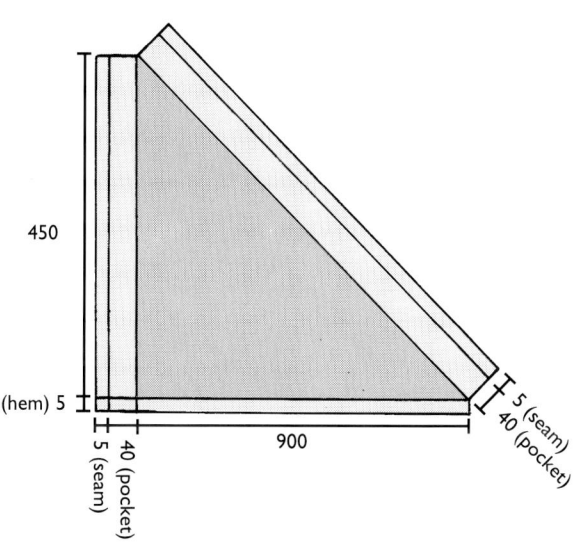

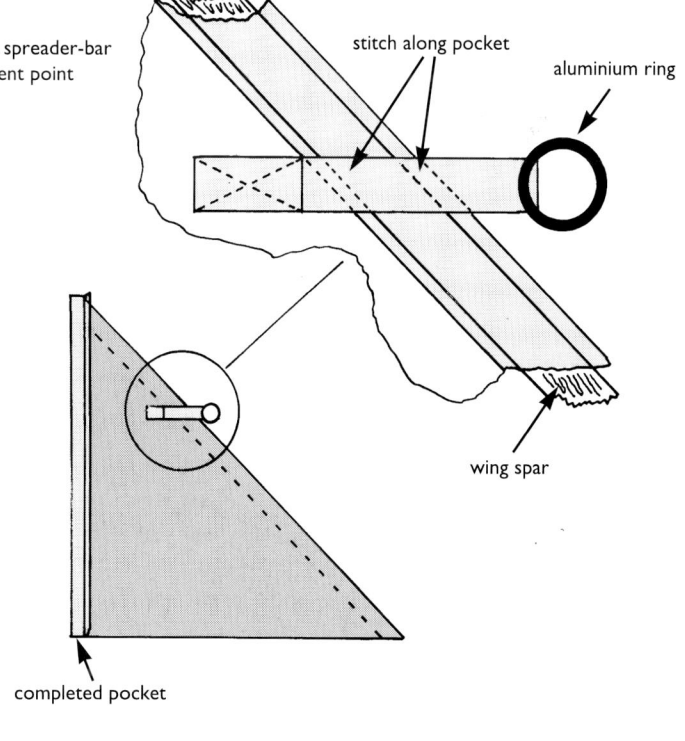

detail of spreader-bar attachment point

stitch along pocket

aluminium ring

wing spar

completed pocket

across the wing. Where this line meets the outer edge of the wing, sew a tape loop and aluminium ring as shown; this will be the attachment point for the spreader bar (cross-spar). Be careful that you do not sew this loop across the pocket.

4   Mark and cut the horizontal panels (Figure 38). Stitch down the hems on the leading and trailing edges, and sew 10 × 100 mm tape loops as shown. These will form the attachment points for the longerons, which will pass through the inner pockets in the wings. As an alternative to the notch-and-bead system, the ends of the outer edges of the longeron pockets could be sewn down.

5   Mark and cut the two lower triangular box sections and hem (Figure 40). Fold in half and sew down the lower pocket. Attach short tape loops to the right-hand panel at both front and rear. The outer loops will provide the attachment points for the lower longeron, while a cord will be passed between the inner ones to hold the cells together. Cut and hem the vertical panels (Figure 39).

6   Assemble the kite (Figure 41). Take the top pair of wings and sew the uppermost horizontal panels in place at the seam formed by the pocket. Turn the wings over and sew the vertical panels to the lower surface (these will connect the

upper wings to the middle set of wings). Take the middle set of wings and sew the two horizontal panels between them. Sew this section to the vertical panels hanging from the upper section. Take the next set of vertical panels and sew these to the lower surface of the central pair of wings. Follow the same procedure with the lower wings, but sew the triangular box sections to the lower surface.

7   Attach short lengths of line and beads to secure the longerons. Cut the longerons to size, notch the ends and fit them into their pockets. Cut the spars for the edges of the wings to size, push into their pockets along the edges of the

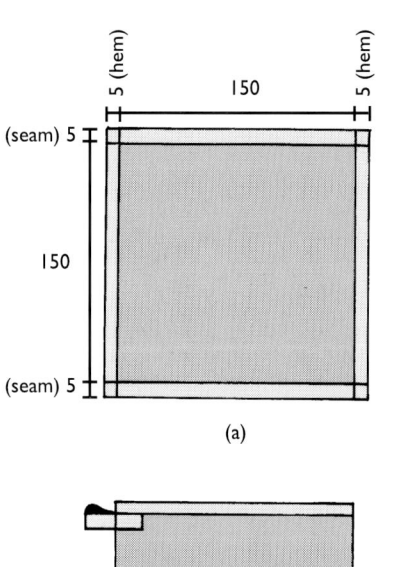

(a)

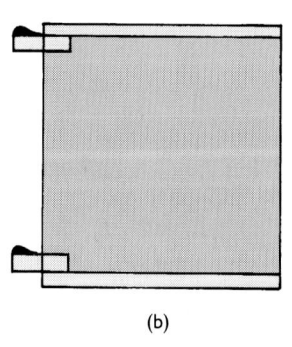

(b)

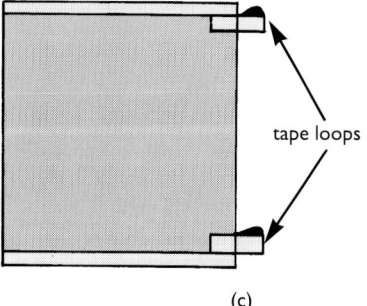

tape loops

(c)

38   Horizontal panel x 6: (a) marking pattern (b) completed front panel (c) completed rear panel

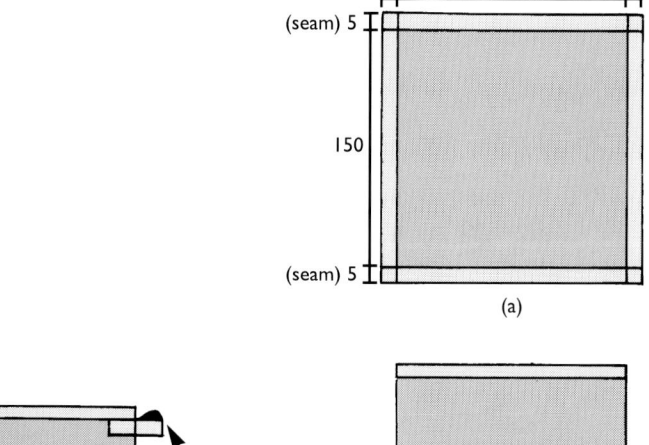

(a)

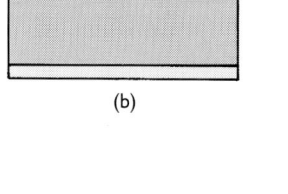

(b)

39   Vertical panel x 8: (a) marking pattern (b) completed panel

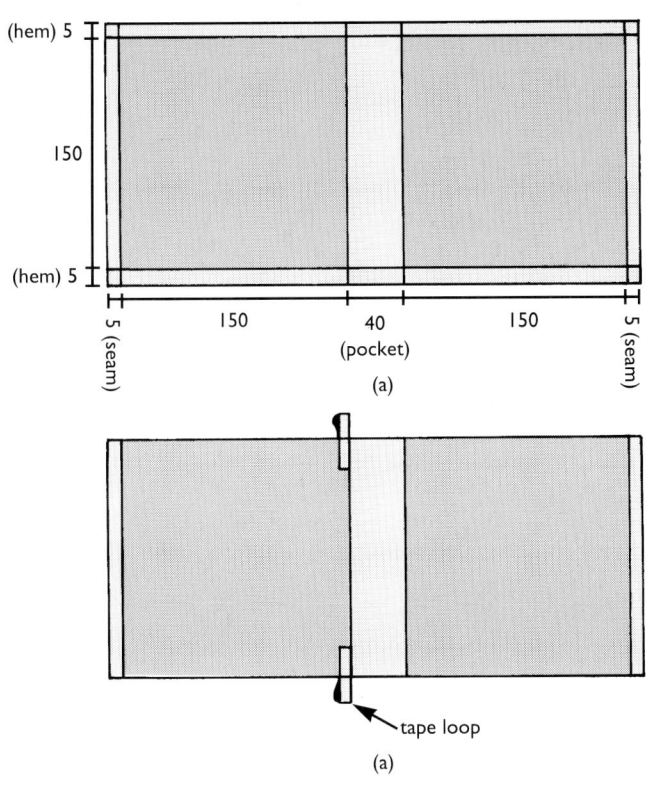

40　Lower panel x 2: (a) marking pattern (b) completed panel

(hem) 5

150

(hem) 5

5 (seam)　150　40 (pocket)　150　5 (seam)

(a)

tape loop

(a)

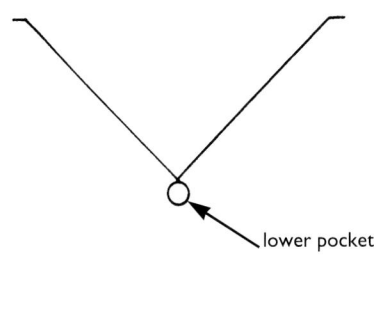

lower pocket

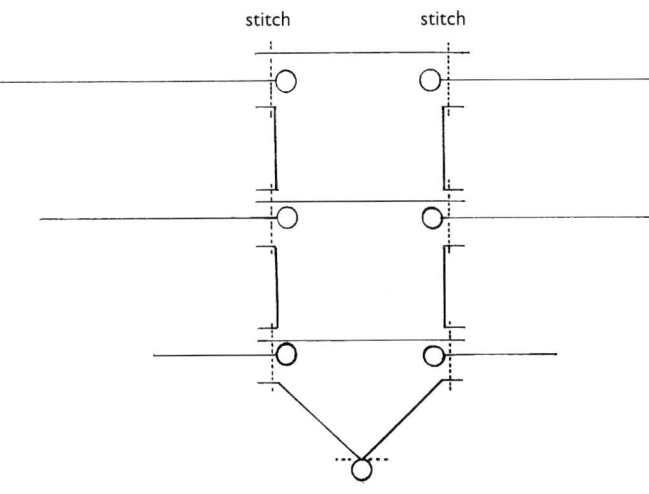

stitch　　stitch

41　Assembly of triple-stack Delta Conyne

wings and sew across the rear edges of the pockets.

8　Cut the spreader bars so that they will stretch the wings tightly. Notch the ends so that they will fit into the aluminium rings located on the wing edges to form the completed kite (Figure 42, overleaf).

9　Form a two-legged bridle on the lower longeron, with the front attachment point at the front edge of the kite and the rear just in front of the rear cell. You may need to move the bridle point depending on the wind. This kite gives quite a pull in a fresh wind and can be flown from 50 kg (100 lb) breaking-strain line.

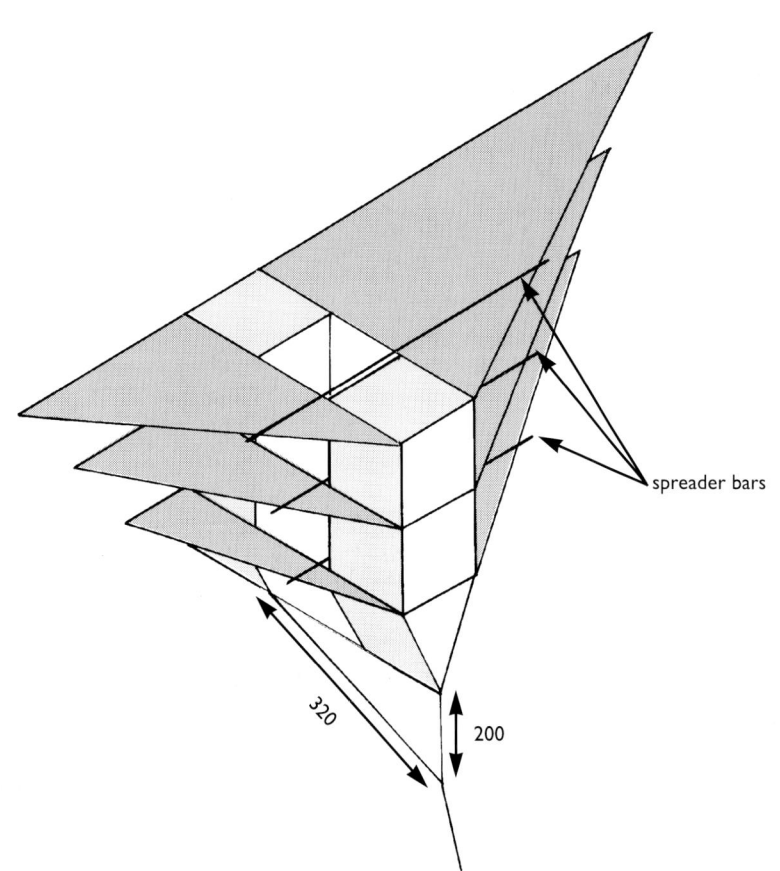

42 Bridling points for triple-stack Delta Conyne

spreader bars

320

200

PETER LYNN TRI-D BOX KITE

Diagrams of this kite tend to be very off-putting, but it is in fact a very simple kite to make and to fly. The required sail tension is achieved by making all the panels with a triangular section in two pieces. If they are made in one piece, there will undoubtedly be unequal stretching, and the result will be a kite which performs badly. An additional bonus in making the panels from two pieces is a strong central seam which further resists stretching.

When making this kite, it is a good idea to use contrasting colours for the box and wing panels, as the shape of the kite tends to be lost when a single colour is used. The basic design can also be the starting point for further development into larger kites such as a three-celled unit. When making such units the size of the longerons and bracing spars must be increased to cope with the extra stress, and a multi-legged bridle should be used.

Peter Lynn Tri-D box kite

MATERIALS

○ Fabric: ripstop nylon, 6 x 1 m
○ Longerons: hardwood dowel, two pieces 9 x 150 mm
○ Vertical bracers: hardwood dowel, two pieces 9 x 120 mm
○ Lower longeron: hardwood dowel, one piece 9 x 70 mm
○ Cross-spars: hardwood dowel, two pieces 12 x 240 mm
○ Thermoplastic or aluminium tubing: internal diameter 9 mm, length 50 mm (two pieces)
○ Dacron tape (optional)
○ PVA adhesive
○ Plastic beads x 12
○ Aluminium ring for bridling point
○ Two strong elastic bands, 'O' rings or short lengths of string

METHOD

I Decide on the colour combinations and mark and cut out the triangular pieces (Figure 43). Hem as necessary and sew the pieces together in pairs, wing section to wing section and box section to box section (use an overlapping or lap seam), to make equilateral 60° triangles with a strong central seam (Figure 44).

2 Sew a tape loop on to the end of each triangular section. This will be stitched on to the central seam and there is no real need to reinforce the point of the triangle to which it is attached, but an optional reinforcement could be made with either ripstop or dacron.

3 Join the equilateral triangles to form pairs (Figure 45). Where the bottoms of the triangles overlap,

sew down along the seams with a zig-zag stitch (Figure 46). Six pairs of these double panels will be needed: two for the upper part of the box, two for the lower part and two for the wings.

4 The kite is actually in two halves, each consisting of an upper and a lower box section and a wing. In this construction method, a pocket is created to hold each of the longerons which run the length of the kite. Some methods do not

have the longerons in pockets, but then they must be tied or secured in some way. A pocket is simple to form and holds the longerons securely in place (Figure 47).

5 To fabricate each of the halves of the kite, sandwich a wing section between the upper and lower box sections with a tape loop, as

43 Marking pattern: (a) wing panel x 8 (b) box panel x 16

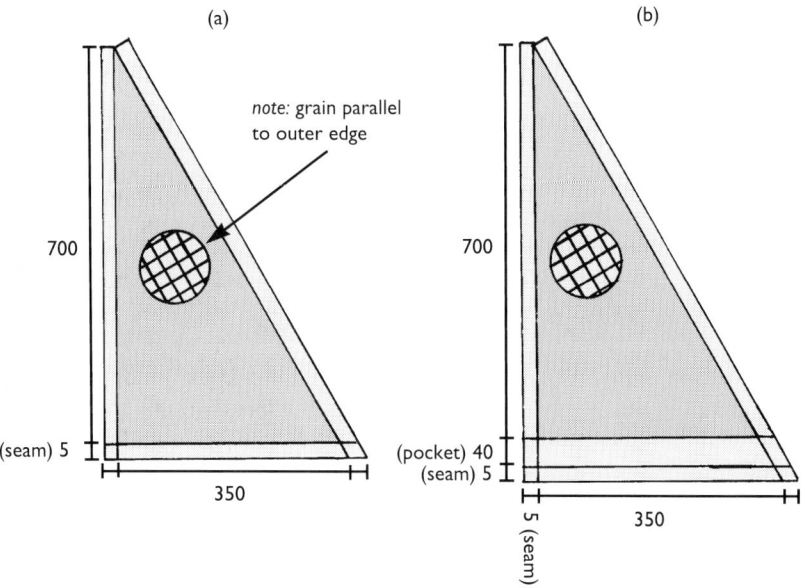

(a)

700

note: grain parallel to outer edge

(seam) 5

350

(b)

700

(pocket) 40
(seam) 5

5 (seam)

350

44 Completed wing panel (the completed box panel can be seen in Figure 45)

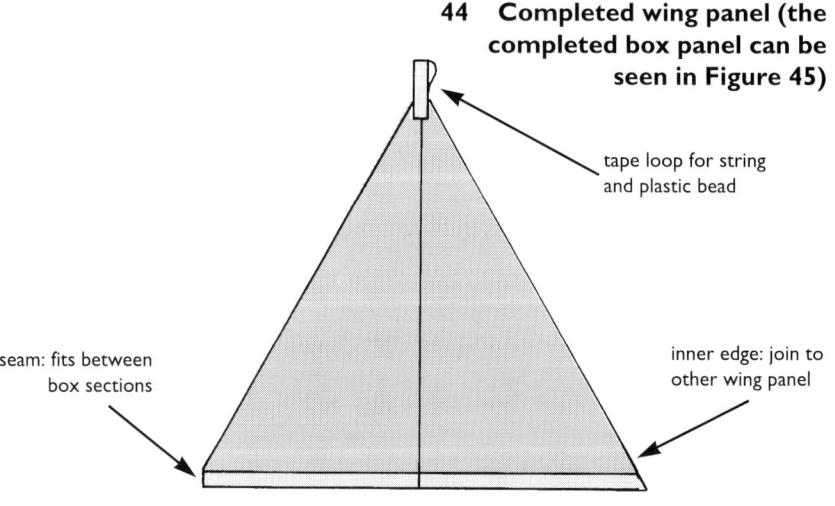

tape loop for string and plastic bead

seam: fits between box sections

inner edge: join to other wing panel

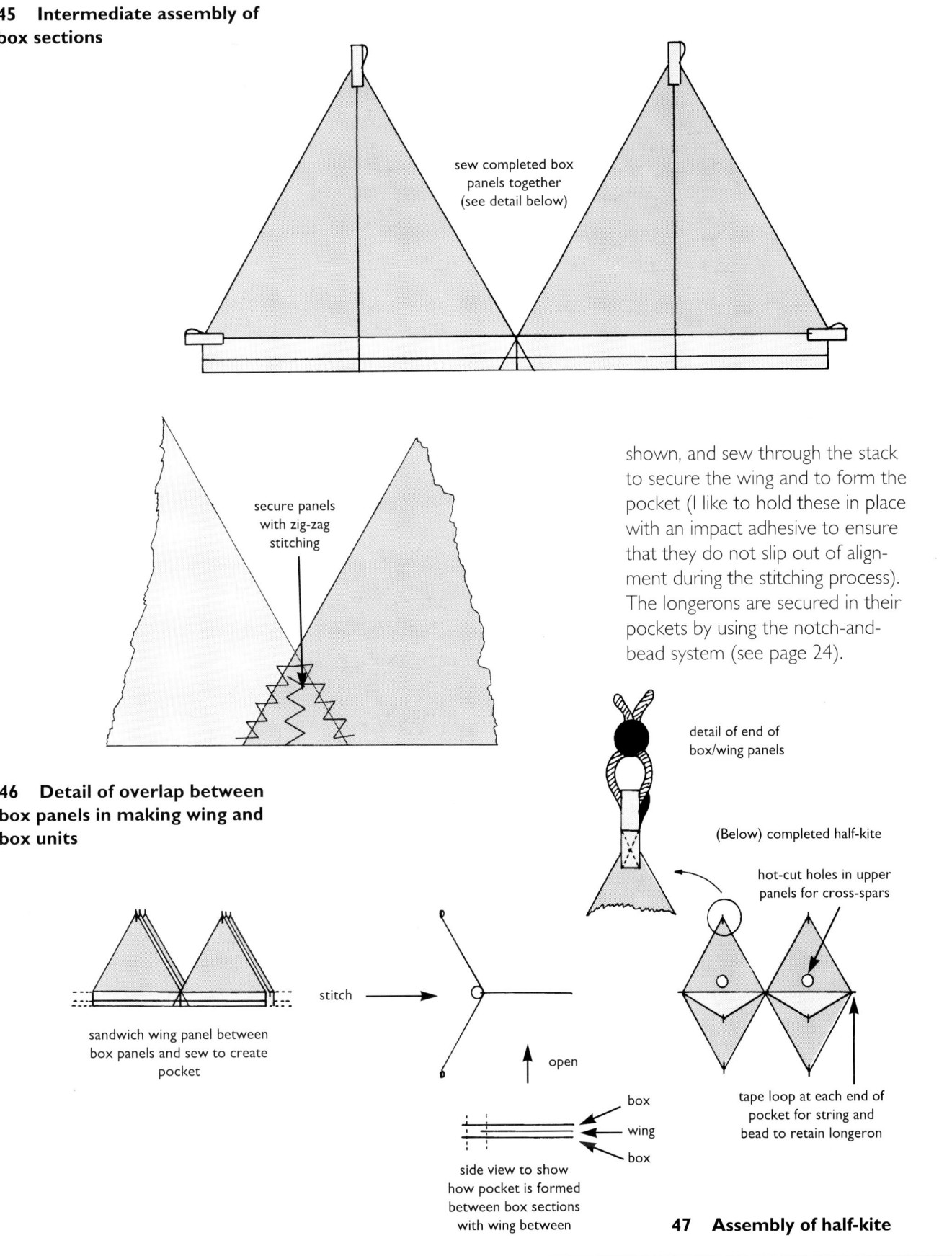

45 Intermediate assembly of box sections

sew completed box panels together (see detail below)

secure panels with zig-zag stitching

46 Detail of overlap between box panels in making wing and box units

sandwich wing panel between box panels and sew to create pocket

stitch

open

box
wing
box

side view to show how pocket is formed between box sections with wing between

shown, and sew through the stack to secure the wing and to form the pocket (I like to hold these in place with an impact adhesive to ensure that they do not slip out of alignment during the stitching process). The longerons are secured in their pockets by using the notch-and-bead system (see page 24).

detail of end of box/wing panels

(Below) completed half-kite

hot-cut holes in upper panels for cross-spars

tape loop at each end of pocket for string and bead to retain longeron

47 Assembly of half-kite

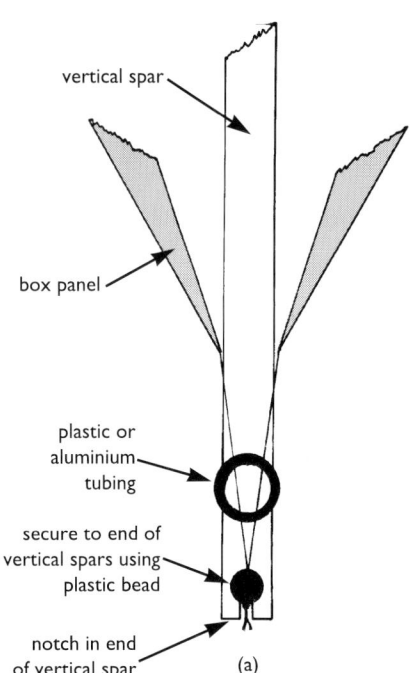

vertical spar

box panel

plastic or aluminium tubing

secure to end of vertical spars using plastic bead

notch in end of vertical spar

(a)

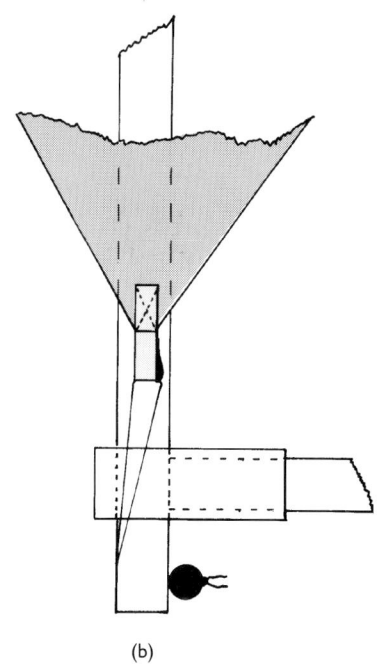

(b)

48 (a) front elevation (b) side elevation

6 The cross-spars which brace the kite have to pass through the box section, and a hole must be made for this purpose. Aesthetically, the spars are better on the upper surface of the kite, so put the holes through the upper panels so that the spars lie on the upper surface of the wings and are out of sight when the kite is flying. Use a soldering iron to hot cut a small hole in each of the upper box sections, along the central seam near to its base. Hot cutting is useful for jobs like this because there is no need to hem the hole.

7 Use the notch-and-bead system (see page 24) to join the two halves of the kite. The left- and right-hand sides are very simply joined by short lengths of line with a plastic bead at their junction. Apart from being simpler than some systems, I also consider this method superior in that it is possible to achieve greater tension in the sails.

8 To erect the kite, push the cross-spars through the kite and locate them at the wing-tips using the notch-and-bead system. Use vertical spars in a single length and hold them together at the centre with a rubber band, an O ring, or simply lash them with a short piece of string.

9 A spar runs along the bottom of this kite between the two vertical spars and a joint is therefore needed. This can be made with suitably drilled aluminium tubing, or plastic tubing with a hole burned through with a soldering iron (Figure 48).

10 In the original design a four-legged bridle, attached to the spars under the wing, was used. Bridles attached to wing spars in this way tend to be cumbersome, however,

49 Completed Peter Lynn Tri-D box kite, flown from fulcrum point below kite

and the kite flies better from a single bridle attached to the fulcrum point (where the front vertical spar meets the lower longeron). The completed kite is shown in Figure 49.

11 Fly the kite on line with a 70 kg (150 lb) breaking strain (this should be greater if conditions are gusty).

FIVE
FURTHER COMPOUND DESIGNS

WINGED BOX KITE

Adding wings to a box kite increases the performance by providing a greater lifting surface, and the wings also remove the need for a jointing system if diagonal bracing spars are used to brace the box sections. Wings also provide an opportunity to add colour to the kite, without breaking up the symmetry of the box sections.

This is a symmetrical kite with four small wings. The kite has a rectangular (not square) section to increase the lifting surface. This gives the kite good performance, and it can be flown in relatively light winds. The longerons and diagonal spars are located in their pockets by a notch in the ends of the spars. These are kept in place by a small plastic bead.

Winged box kite

MATERIALS

○ Fabric: ripstop nylon, 3·5 x 1 m
○ Longerons: hardwood dowel, four pieces 6 x 1300 mm
○ Diagonal spars: hardwood dowel, four pieces 9 x 1200 mm
○ Cardboard
○ PVA adhesive
○ Plastic beads x 16
○ Aluminium ring for bridling point

METHOD

1   Cut out cardboard templates for the wing and panel sections and cut the fabric (Figure 50 a–c).

2   Stitch down the hems around the edges of the wings. Fold over the pocket allowance and stitch down to form the pocket. Cut out 16 ripstop circles 100 mm in diameter, fold them in half and use them to reinforce the corners of the wings where the tape loops will be attached. Cut away any reinforcement which protrudes past the edges of the wing. Form tape loops measuring 10 x 100 mm from four layers of ripstop and stitch to the wings. To each of these loops, affix a short length of flying line and a plastic bead. Cut the pockets and stitch to the surface of the wing, which will face outwards. The completed wing section is shown in Figure 51 (overleaf).

3   Stitch down the hems on the box sections and cut two semi-circular holes to accommodate the diagonal spars in the larger panels (which will form the upper and lower surfaces). Stitch the completed panels to the wing sections so that each wing section is sandwiched between a vertical and a horizontal panel (Figures 52 and 53, overleaf). Secure the material with adhesive to ensure that it does not slip during sewing. The joint can be made with the join on the inside or the outside (the inside gives a more polished appearance).

50   Marking pattern: (a) side panel x 4 (b) top/bottom panel x 4 (c) wing x 4

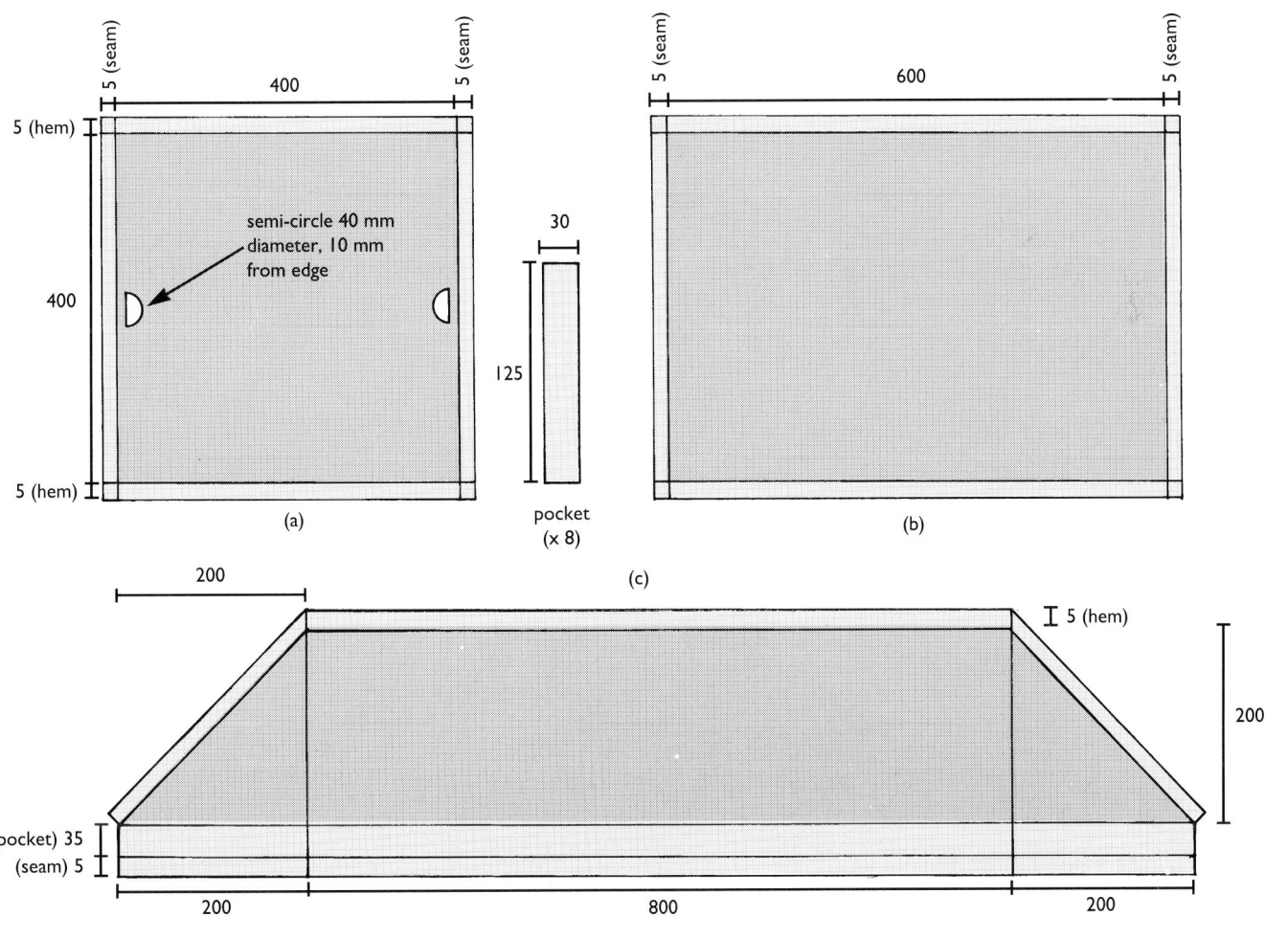

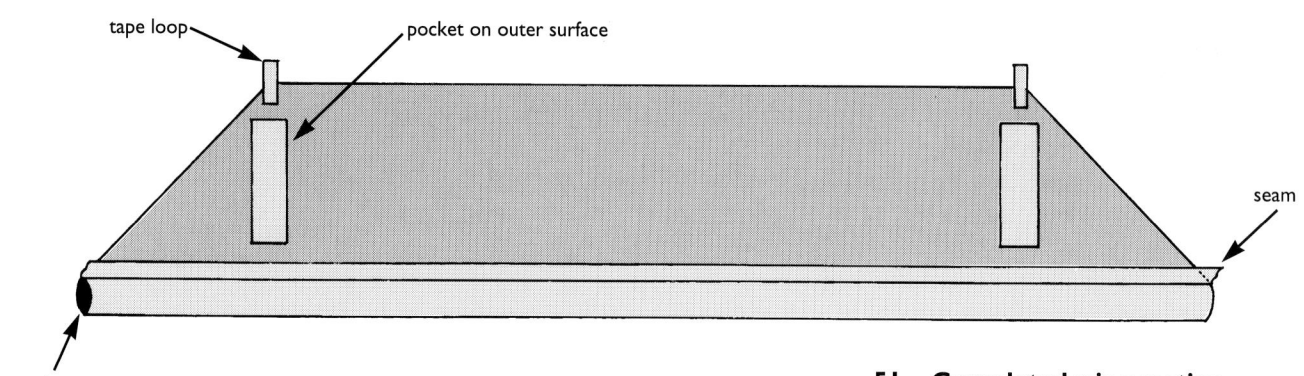

tape loop

pocket on outer surface

seam

pocket

51 Completed wing section

4 Once you have stitched the panels to the wings, stitch a tape loop at each outside corner, where the vertical panel meets the wing. A loop of line and a plastic bead can then be attached. Cut notches about 5 mm deep in the ends of the longerons and fit them into the pocket, securing them in position with the tape loops. Fine adjustments to the length of the line in the tape loops can be made to give a tight fit.

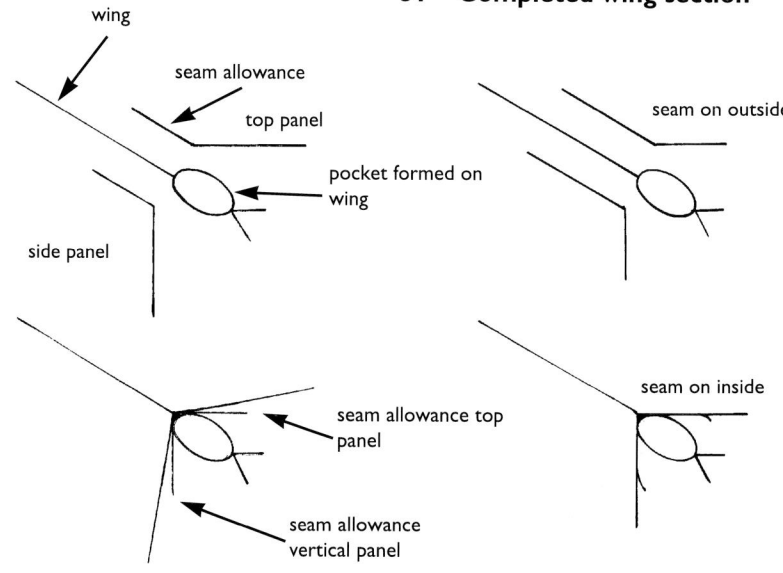

wing

seam allowance

top panel

seam on outside

side panel

pocket formed on wing

seam allowance top panel

seam on inside

seam allowance vertical panel

52 Methods of forming corner seam

5 Assemble the kite by inserting the diagonal spars. Again, fine adjustments to the line in the tape loops can be made. Attach the bridle lines to the tape loops on the lower front panel (where the longerons are secured) to fly the kite from a two-legged bridle. Use a bridle line three metres long, forming a loop at the central point to give well-behaved flight.

6 The kite should be flown from line with a 70 kg (150 lb) breaking strain.

seam formed on outside

stitch

wing

top panel

53 Assembly of winged box kite

Box Delta

The Box Delta has the square box-kite configuration and is fitted with a delta wing. In many ways this is superior to the Delta Conyne (see page 16) as the four-sided box gives much greater stability than the three-sided one. This box delta has double sets of internal bracers, for both front and rear cells, which gives better rigidity than a single set of centrally positioned bracers. When two sets of bracers are used for each cell, lighter wood can be substituted.

A Delta Conyne kite can be made by following the instructions given for the Conyne kite (see pages 52–4), but using a delta wing of the type shown for the Box Delta instead of the normal Conyne wing.

Box Delta

MATERIALS

○ Fabric: ripstop nylon, 4·5 x 1 m
○ Longerons: hardwood dowel, four pieces 9 x 1300 mm
○ Diagonal spars: hardwood dowel, eight pieces 6 x 550 mm
○ Cross-spar: hardwood dowel, 9 x 1500 mm
○ Elastic bands x 4
○ Plastic fuel line (or other plastic tubing): internal diameter 6 mm, length 500 mm
○ PVA adhesive
○ Plastic beads x 8
○ Aluminium ring for bridling point

METHOD

I   Mark and cut out the delta wing (Figure 54). The design on the kite wing was produced by sewing together three strips of material and then sewing the panel down around the outside (it helps if the panel is lightly glued with a stick adhesive while you are doing this). The black material behind the panel was then cut away, creating a stained-glass-window effect which is most striking when the sun shines on it from behind.

2   Tape loops must be fitted to the delta wing to locate the spreader bar which supports the wings. There are several possible positions for these loops: just behind the line of the rear cell; in the centre of the kite; or just in front of the rear cells. I prefer the latter position as it seems to maintain the shape of the wing better. When the loops are sewn into place, attach a plastic bead to each using a length of line, to form the location points for the spreader bar. If you wish, you may delay sewing these loops until after the wings have been sewn to the cells.

3   Cut out the front and rear cells (Figure 55a–b) and stitch the hems down along the long edges. The assembly of the kite is shown in Figure 56.

4   Lay out the two completed front and rear cells with their outer surface uppermost, and stitch on the two wings as shown. Turn the kite over and stitch the three inner sets of pockets into place; the fourth set of pockets is formed by the allowances on the outer edges of the panels.

5   Stitch tape loops to the outer edges where the pockets will be formed, to hold loops of line and plastic beads. They can also be sewn to the inner edges which do not touch the wings, so that lines can be fitted to hold the kite taut when assembled.

6   Cut the lengths of 6 mm dowel which go into the wing pockets and give each a couple of turns in a pencil sharpener to remove the edges. Fit into the pockets and sew down along the trailing edge.

7   Cut longerons to match the dimensions of the completed kite and notch the ends as appropriate.

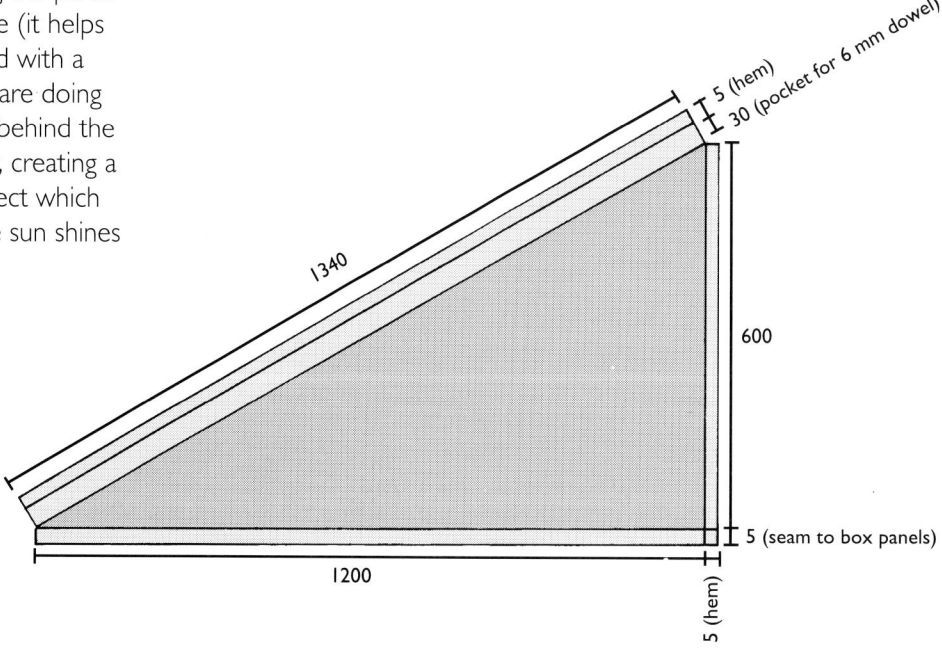

54   Wing section x 2

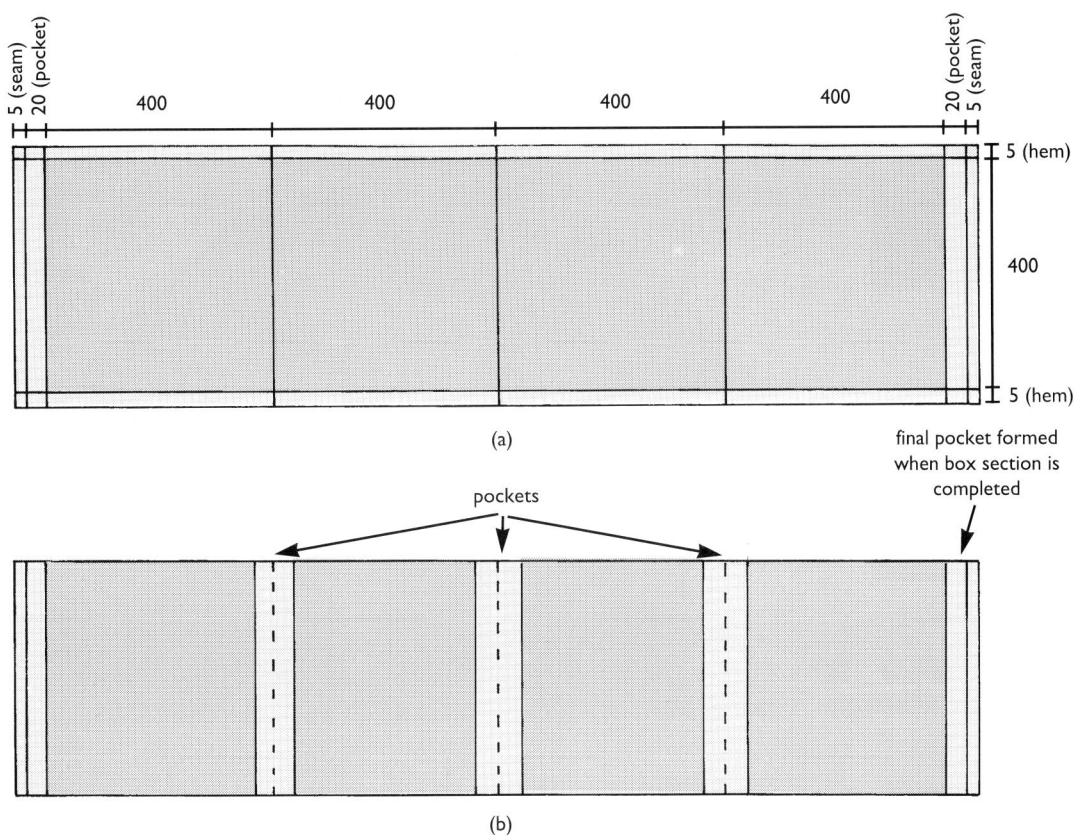

5 (seam)
20 (pocket)

400   400   400   400

20 (pocket)
5 (seam)

5 (hem)

400

5 (hem)

(a)

pockets

final pocket formed
when box section is
completed

(b)

Cut the plastic joints as described on page 31 and fit them to the longerons as you put them into their pockets. Plastic joints are fitted to each longeron at the inner and outer edges of the panels.

8 Make four sets of diagonals and join each pair at the centre with an elastic band cut from an old cycle inner tube. These are fitted to give the box sections their shape. Cut the spreader bar to fit the beads, and push into place between the locating beads to spread the wings (Figures 57 and 58, overleaf).

9 Fly the kite from a two-legged bridle (front leg 760 mm, rear leg 1240 mm) on 75 kg (150 lb) breaking-strain line.

55   Box section x 2: (a) marking pattern (b) completed section

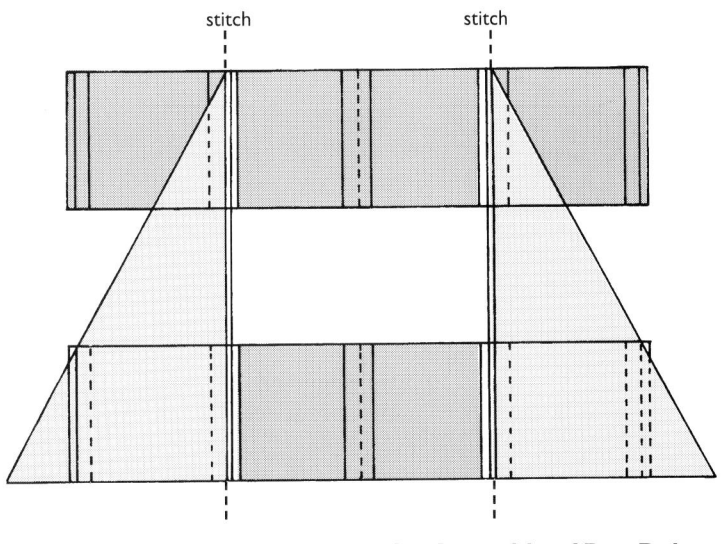

stitch   stitch

56   Assembly of Box Delta

57 Completed Box Delta, showing bracers and spreader-bar attachment

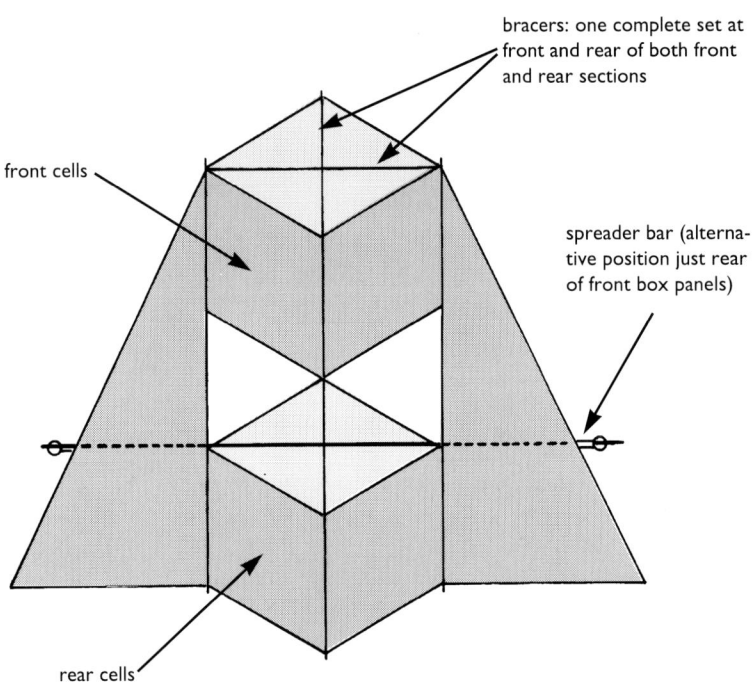

bracers: one complete set at front and rear of both front and rear sections

front cells

spreader bar (alternative position just rear of front box panels)

rear cells

58 Cut-away diagram showing front and rear bracers to each cell

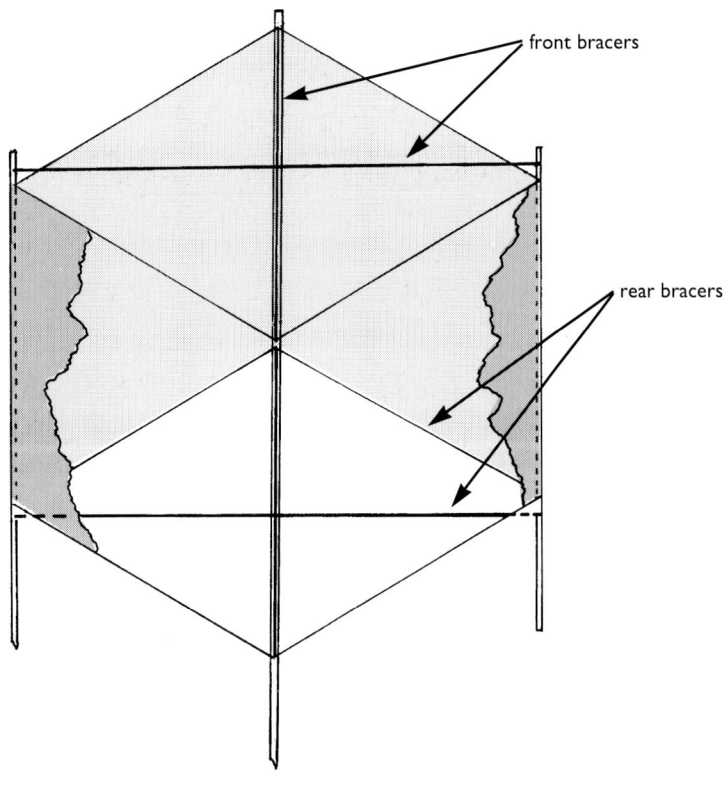

front bracers

rear bracers

THREE-CELLED WINGED BOX KITE

Most box kites have two cells separated by a central space, but it is possible to increase the number to three or more. This produces a kite which is longer and narrower: that is, it has a lower-aspect ratio. One of the consequences is that the kite has less lift, but this is compensated by greater stability. The kite described here has three cells and four wings for extra lift, and is a very stable kite even in relatively strong winds. This design can easily be adapted to a two-celled box.

MATERIALS

○ Fabric: ripstop nylon, 5·5 x 1 m
○ Longerons: hardwood dowel, four pieces 9 x 1600 mm
○ Diagonal spars: two pieces 9 x 1150 mm; four pieces 9 x 800 mm
○ Plastic beads x 20
○ Aluminium ring for bridling point

METHOD

The basic principle is that the pockets are made on the wings, to which the rectangular cells are stitched. The kite is braced centrally by diagonal spars running to the wing-tips and to the inner edge of the outer panels.

1 Cut out the wings (Figure 59, overleaf). Each wing is made from two sections, with the weave

Three-celled winged box kite

75

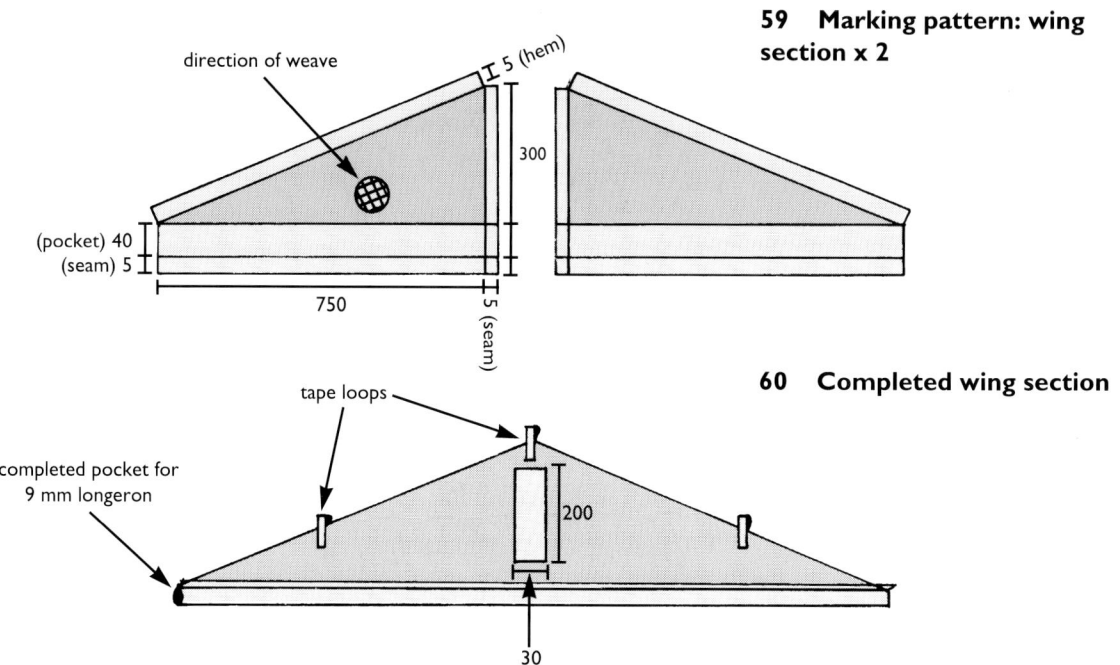

59   Marking pattern: wing section x 2

direction of weave

5 (hem)

300

(pocket) 40
(seam) 5

750

5 (seam)

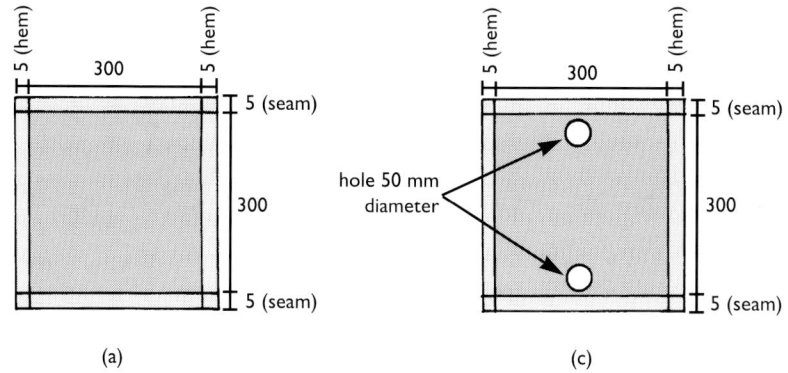

60   Completed wing section

tape loops

completed pocket for
9 mm longeron

200

30

parallel to the outer edge. In theory the wing could be cut from a single piece of fabric, but this creates an unfavourable alignment on the weave which causes stretching. Sew the two sections together, and sew a hem around the outside.

2   Sew three tape loops (10 × 100 mm, made from four thicknesses of ripstop) at the central point, and at points 300 mm from the pocket and projected vertically on to the outer edge of the wing. Fit all the tape points with plastic beads attached to lengths of line (see Figure 14 on page 40). Sew a pocket for the central diagonal spars. Create the pocket by folding the pocket allowance over and stitching it down (Figure 60).

3   Mark and cut out the panels which will form the box sections (Figure 61a–d). Cut holes in the centre panels with a soldering iron to allow the central diagonal spars to pass through them. Sew down the hems on all the panels.

5 (hem)   300   5 (hem)

5 (seam)

300

5 (seam)

(a)

5 (hem)   300   5 (hem)

5 (seam)

hole 50 mm
diameter

300

5 (seam)

(c)

(b)

(d)

61   Side panel x 8: (a) marking pattern (b) completed panel. Centre panel x 4: (c) marking pattern (d) completed panel

4   Assemble the kite by sewing the panels to the wings along the line of the pockets. Sew tape loops to the outer edges of the outer panels, to form points of attachment for line and loops which will hold the longerons.

5   Cut the four longerons to size and notch the ends. Push them into the pockets which run along the wings and locate them using the notch-and-bead system (see page 24). Cut the two long central diagonals to size and use them to erect the kite, and fit the shorter diagonals to give extra rigidity. The completed kite is shown in Figure 62.

6   The easiest way to fly the kite is from a two-legged bridle attached to the lower front corners of the kite. Use line with a breaking strain of about 70 kg (150 lb).

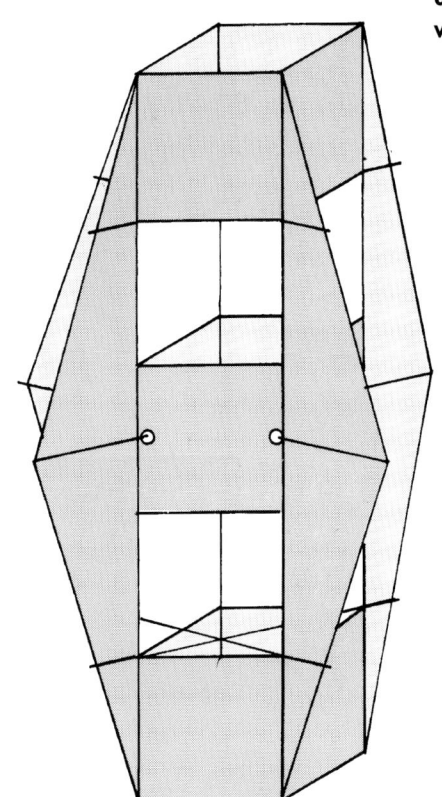

62   Completed three-celled winged box kite

THE CODY WAR KITE

The Cody war kite is one of the finest of all kites, whose name was derived from the fact that Cody tried to sell his kite to the army and navy for possible use as a man-lifter in times of war. The war kite was also used as a signal kite, and as an instrument for lifting meteorological instruments. It was derived from the early compound Cody kite, but is an altogether more rigid structure, with very taut lifting surfaces.

The constructions described here are not intended to be exact replicas of the originals, but modern representations using the materials available today. The use of ripstop nylon as opposed to silk or canvas on the originals largely reduces the need to give all the panels a concave face, as good tension can be obtained using straight sides. However, curved edges may be used if desired.

Even with considerable simplification, the Cody designs are not the easiest kites to make, and I would suggest that you do not attempt them until you have gained some practice with other types of box kite. If you wish to make a large war kite, it is a good idea to make a small model first to learn the technique of making this type of kite.

Cody war kite

MATERIALS

○ Fabric: ripstop nylon, 5 × 1 m
○ Longerons: hardwood dowel, four pieces 9 × 1150 mm
○ Longerons in central panels: hardwood dowel, four pieces 9 × 370 mm
○ Front diagonals: hardwood dowel, two pieces 9 × 2000 mm
○ Rear diagonals: hardwood dowel, two pieces 9 × 1400 mm
○ Wing bracers: square-section hardwood, two pieces 6 × 6 × 450 mm
○ PVA adhesive
○ Dacron tape (optional)
○ Elastic bands × 2 or string
○ Plastic beads × 20
○ Line tensioners × 6
○ Aluminium ring for bridling point

Note:
This design is based on a 350 mm square cell, which gives a wing-span of about 2000 mm. For flying in heavier wind, the 9 mm cross-spars could be replaced by thicker dowel, fibreglass tubing or bamboo. The longerons can be conveniently located in their pockets using the notch-and-bead method (see page 24), or they could be tied to the kite panels with a length of string as in the original models. The general structure of the war kite is shown in Figures 63–6.

METHOD

The original Cody kites were very strongly built with around seventy pieces of reinforcement. For normal recreational flying, the sparring and reinforcement can be considerably reduced.

1 At the fabrication stage, sew reinforcements to the corners of the panels and other vulnerable points (see Figure 79 on page 88). These are made by cutting circles of ripstop 150 mm in diameter,

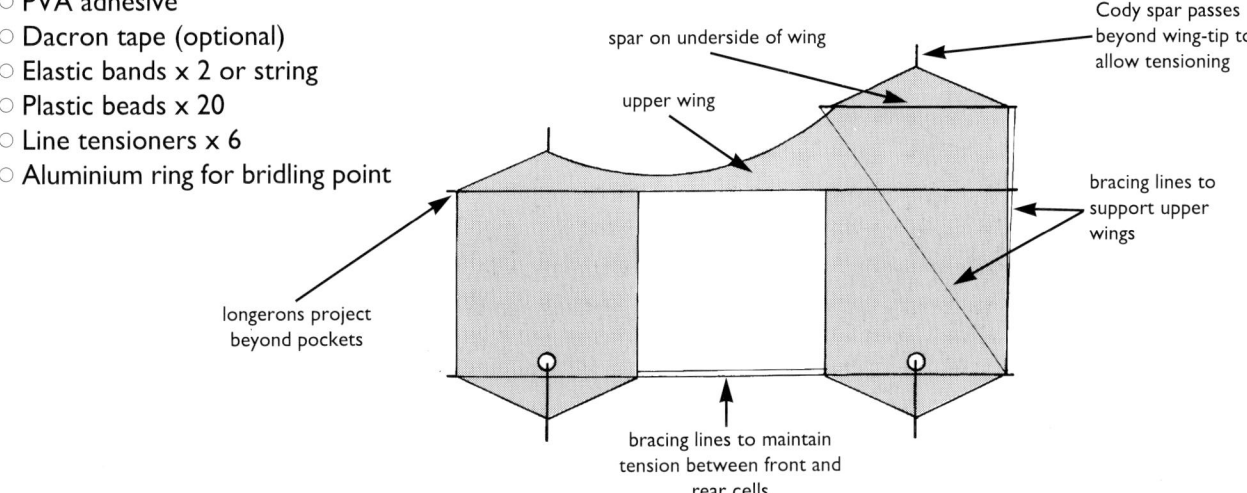

63   Side elevation of Cody war kite

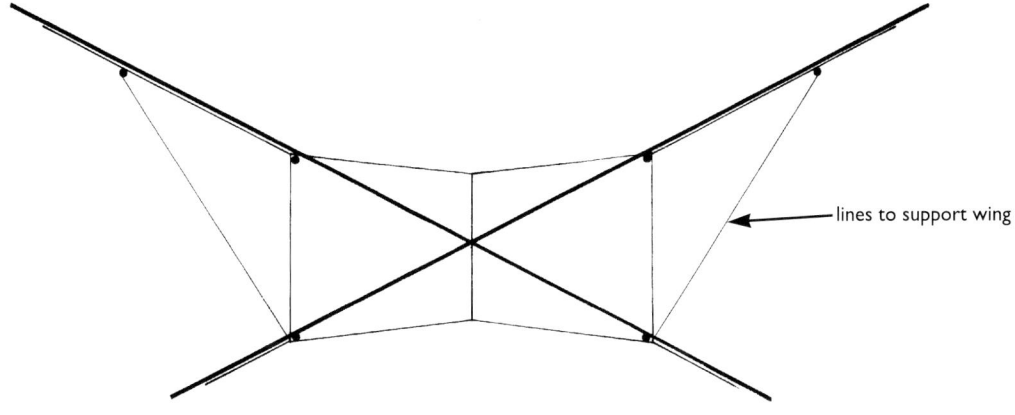

64   Front elevation

65   Upper surface

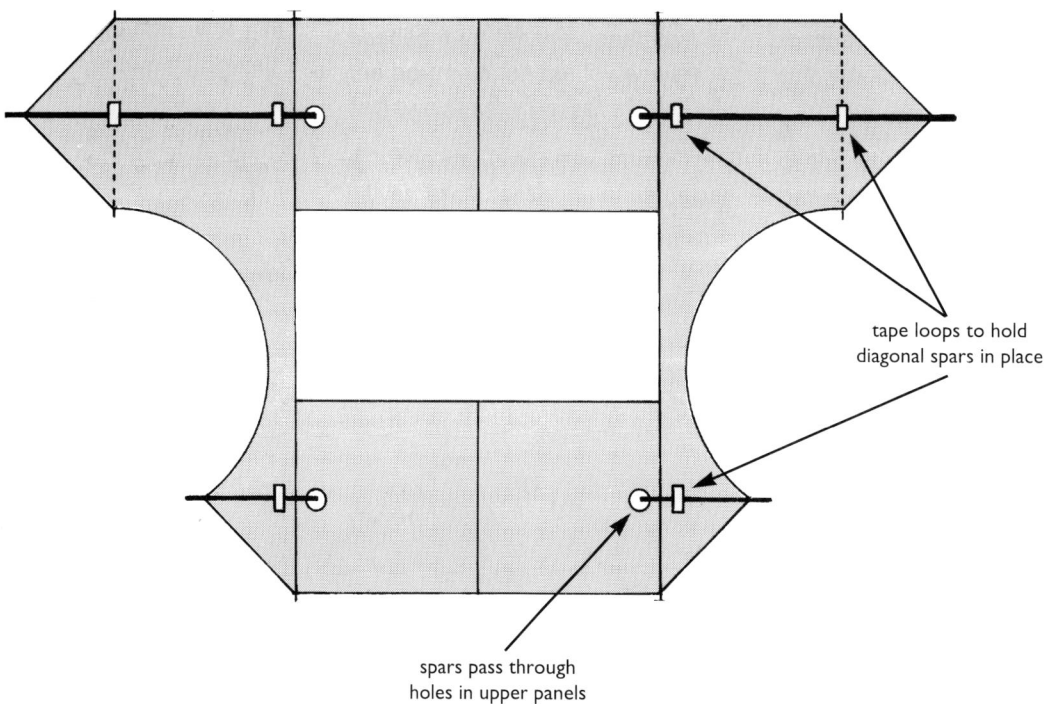

tape loops to hold
diagonal spars in place

spars pass through
holes in upper panels

66   Lower surface

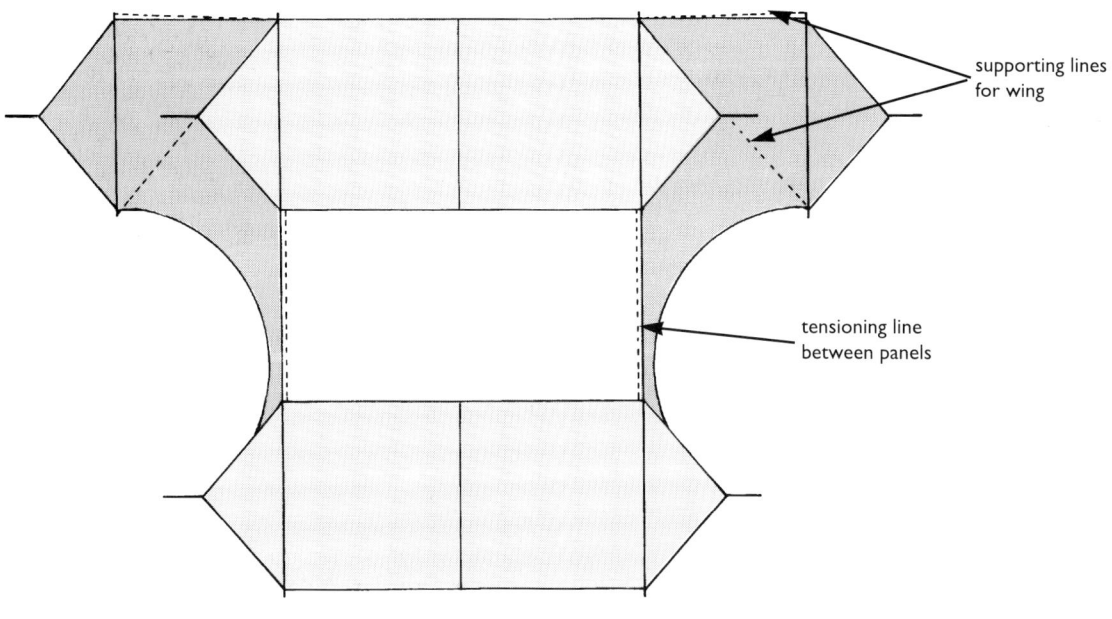

supporting lines
for wing

tensioning line
between panels

folding them in half and gluing the halves together to produce a double-thickness semi-circular section. Cut this in half to make two corner-reinforcement pieces. Glue these into the corners of the panel and stitch down. Instead of circles it is equally good to use triangular-shaped reinforcement pieces. Dacron tape could also be used.

2 The wings are the most difficult part. Mark out the main body of the wing (Figures 67 and 68), but do not cut it out immediately. The curved edge of the wing will need to be reinforced, and this can best be done using a strip made from four thicknesses of ripstop or strong binding tape. If the strip of material is cut at an angle of 45° across the fabric, it will stretch around curves more easily. Glue this in position on the inside of the curve on the upper wing surface and sew into position. Then cut out the wing. If the curve is cut

before sewing on the binding, it is difficult to stitch the binding on and the cut section tends to stretch.

3 Next, cut out the pointed sections on the wing-tips (Figure 69, overleaf), with the direction of the grain as shown in Figure 68, and stitch together. If you cut the points to the wings in one piece, the weave will not be parallel to the edge and the wings will stretch. Stretching is always a problem in kites, but in a highly tensioned kite such as the Cody, it could be particularly troublesome. When you

have made the wing-tip section, sew down the hems along the two outer edges before joining it to the main wing section.

4 Sew the other hems around the outer edges of the wing, then fold over the pocket allowance and sew down to complete the pocket for the upper longeron. Using four thicknesses of ripstop, sew on three tapes to hold the beads: one at the extreme point of the kite, and the other two at the edges where the point was joined to the main wing body.

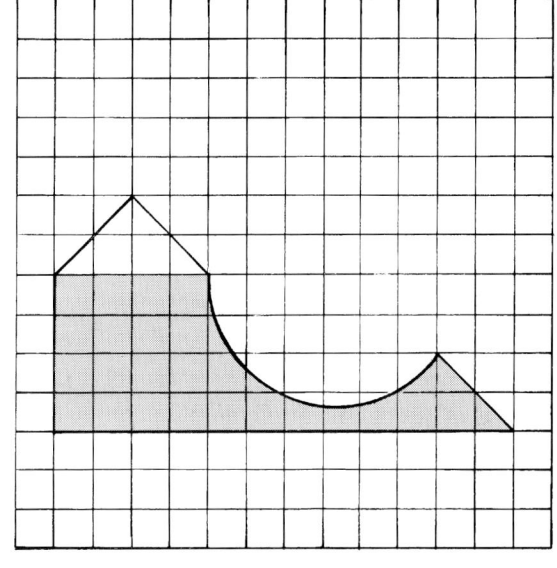

67   Pattern for basic wing (after affixing point, which is constructed separately). The curve may be drawn with a large compass

68   Marking pattern for wing

point constructed from two halves: note that the grain runs parallel to the edges

5 (seam)

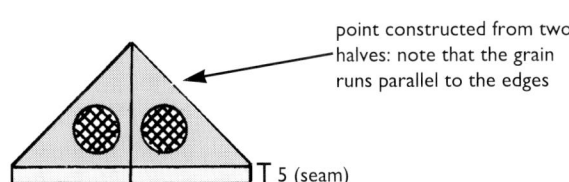

350

350

I 5 (seam)

5 (hem)

40 (pocket)

5 (hem)

5 (hem)

1050

5 (hem)

stitch

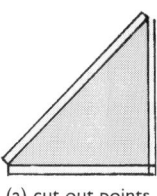

(a) cut out points

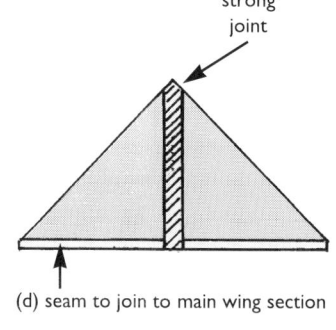

(b) lay points on top of each other
and stitch along line shown

69   Assembly of wing-tips

hems

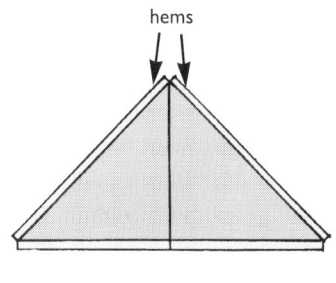

(c) open out and stitch down hems

strong
joint

(d) seam to join to main wing section

5   Sew the pocket for the spar which braces the wing on to the underside of the wing. To restrain the diagonal spars, sew tape loops to the upper surface of the wing. Pockets were used on the original kites, but the sewing of the pockets can weaken the wing, which is under great stress when tensioned. The completed wing section and details of the wing-tip are shown in Figures 70–2.

6   Mark out the side, upper, lower and centre panels (Figures 73–6, overleaf) and cut out, leaving hems and seam allowances as appropriate. For each of the panels, sew the hems as shown and cut the holes through which the diagonal spars will pass (preferably using a soldering iron to prevent fraying). It is a good idea to sew a reinforcement patch around the hole before it is

cut: the soldering iron will then weld the layers of material together.

7   The centre panel has spars at the top and bottom to give extra rigidity. Form the pockets to accommodate these spars from the pocket allowances on the inner edges of the upper and lower panels. Sew tape loops on to the centre panel to provide attachment points for beads. These fit into notches in the end of the 9 mm spars, which in turn fit into the pockets. The completed upper and lower panels are shown in Figure 77 on page 86, and the same reinforcements should be used on the centre and side panels.

8   The wings, top, bottom, side and centre sections must now be stitched together to form the kite (Figure 78, page 86). Start with the

centre sections and sew them on to the upper and lower panels. Next sew on the side panels, forming the bottom pockets in the process. Stitch the pockets so that the pocket is on the inside.

9   To complete the box sections, sew the side and upper panels on to the completed wing panel, on which the upper pocket has already been formed.

10   Sew further tape loops at each of the four corners (front and rear), to the horizontal panels near the main pockets. These will form attachment points for the long-erons, and on the inside of the bottom panels will allow tensioning cords to be fitted between the front and rear cells. Sew these loops to the vertical panels. Attach the rest of the beads to their

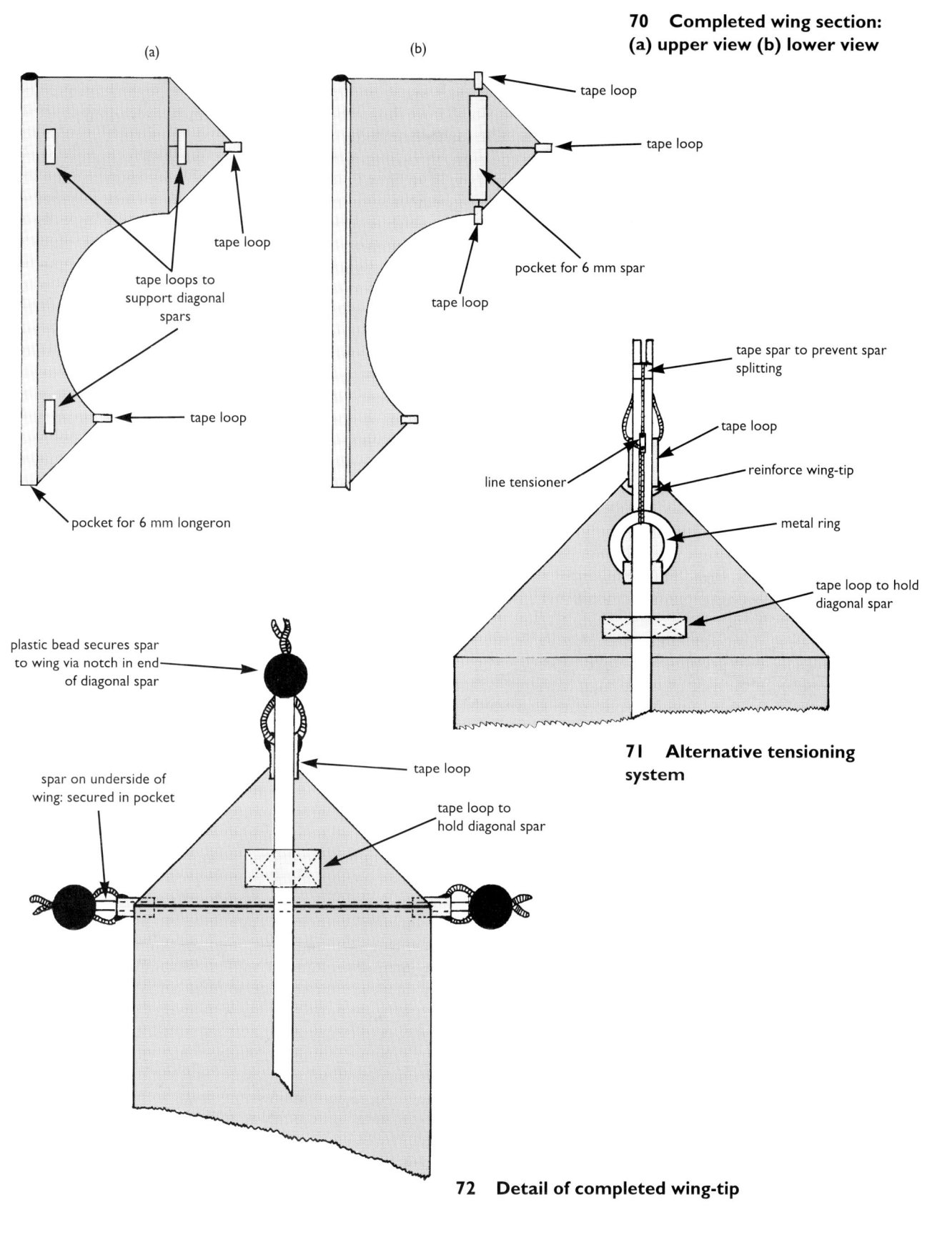

**70 Completed wing section:
(a) upper view (b) lower view**

(a)

(b)

tape loop

tape loop

tape loop

tape loops to
support diagonal
spars

pocket for 6 mm spar

tape loop

tape loop

pocket for 6 mm longeron

tape spar to prevent spar
splitting

tape loop

line tensioner

reinforce wing-tip

metal ring

tape loop to hold
diagonal spar

**71 Alternative tensioning
system**

plastic bead secures spar
to wing via notch in end
of diagonal spar

tape loop

spar on underside of
wing: secured in pocket

tape loop to
hold diagonal spar

72 Detail of completed wing-tip

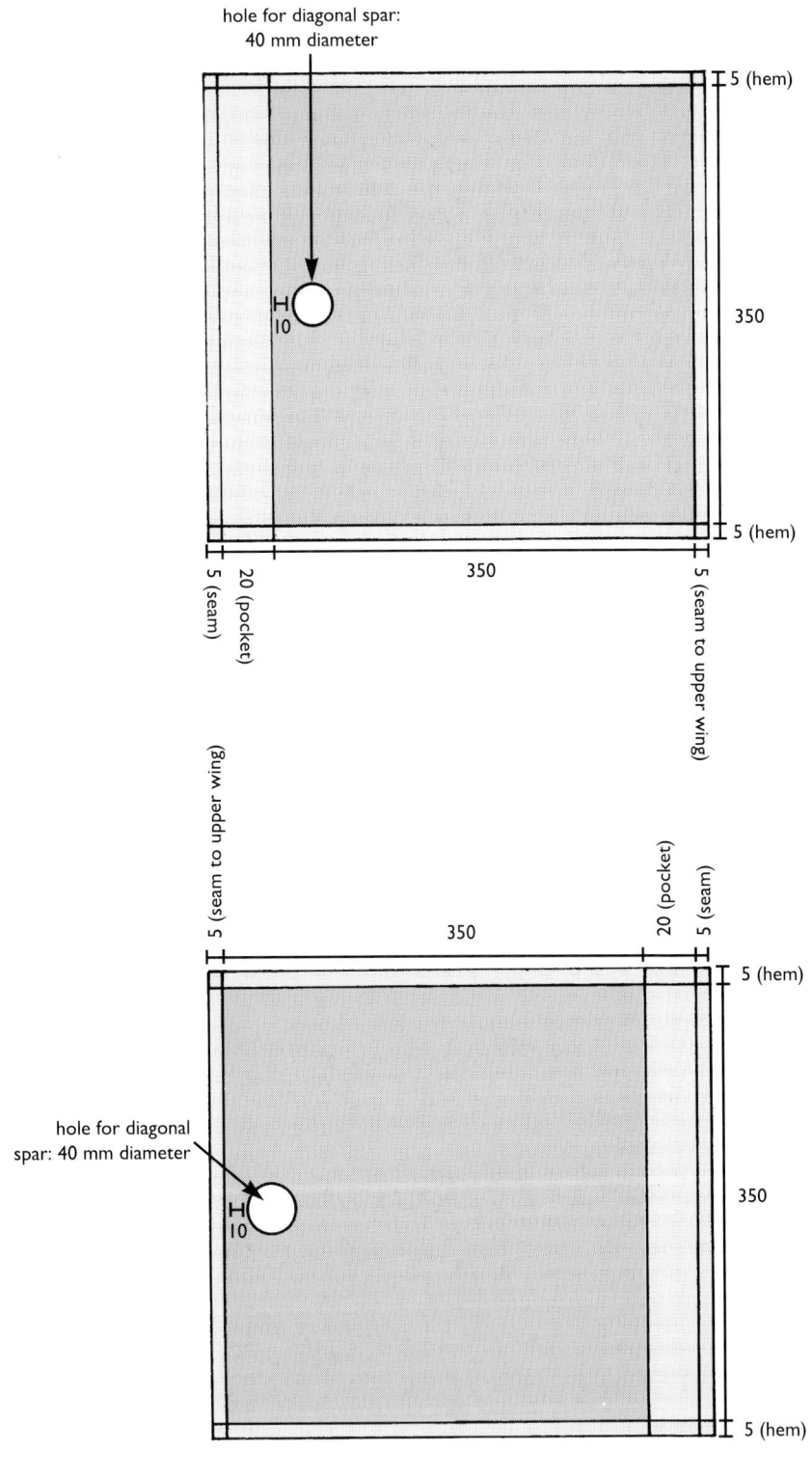

73   Marking pattern for side panel x 4

hole for diagonal spar:
40 mm diameter

5 (hem)

350

H
10

5 (hem)

5 (seam)
20 (pocket)
350
5 (seam to upper wing)

5 (seam to upper wing)
350
20 (pocket)
5 (seam)

5 (hem)

hole for diagonal
spar: 40 mm diameter

350

H
10

5 (hem)

74   Marking pattern for upper panel x 4

anchorage points, and cut the longerons to size so that they are a tight fit. Cut the longerons slightly longer than necessary so that you can reduce them to exactly the right size for the kite. At the crossing points the longerons may be linked to each other with a strong elastic band, or tied together with string.

11   Link the front and rear cells at the lower edges, using tensioning lines which can be adjusted with line tensioners. The wings are supported by lines attached to the front edges of the lower longerons.

12   The Cody war kite may be flown from a two-legged bridle attached to the front of the lower longerons, or from a four-legged bridle. For the two-legged bridle, take the size of the box sections as one unit, and make the front legs four units long. Then attach the rear legs to the longerons in front of the rear cells and to a loop one unit down the front legs of the bridle. By adjusting the length of the rear bridle lines, the pull on the kite can be varied.

75 Marking pattern for lower panel x 4

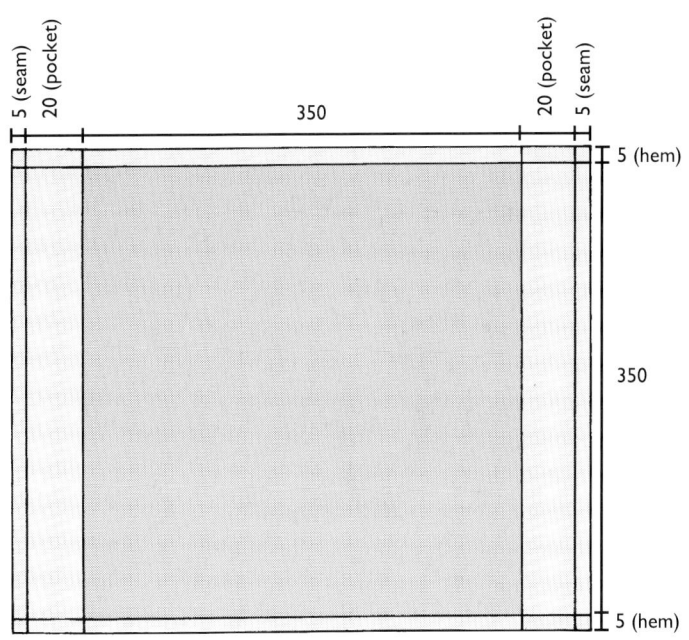

13   The advantages of the two-legged bridle are that the kite will fly with a relatively light pull and will be self-adjusting, but to get the maximum amount of lift you will need to use a four-legged bridle. First measure out enough line to make a two-legged bridle from the front of the kite, so that each leg is four times as long as each cell. Leave enough line to tie to the front longerons, and enough to tie a small loop a quarter of the way down each leg of the completed bridle. Take additional bridle lines from the lower longerons, just in front of the rear cells, to the small loops in the front legs of the kite. These lines need to be about three units (ie. three times the length of the cells). At three units the kite will be flying the front legs only, but the rear bridle lines can be progressively shortened to make the pull on the kite increase, until you eventually reach the point of maximum pull. If the rear lines are shortened too much, the kite will simply stall and will not fly.

14   You will need to fly a Cody of these dimensions on a line with a breaking strain of 70 kg (150 lb).

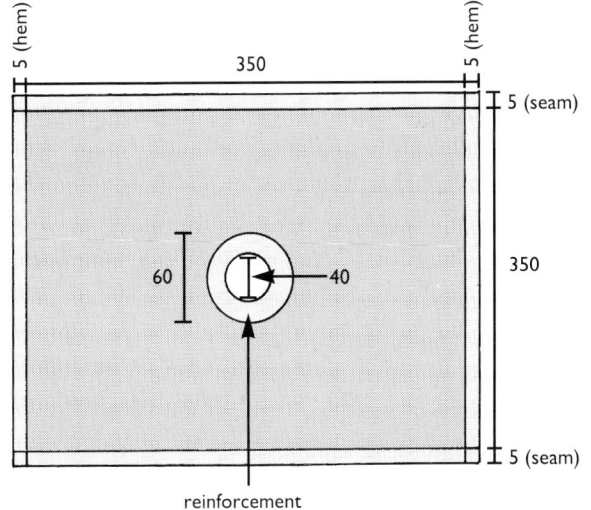

reinforcement

76 Marking pattern for centre panel x 2

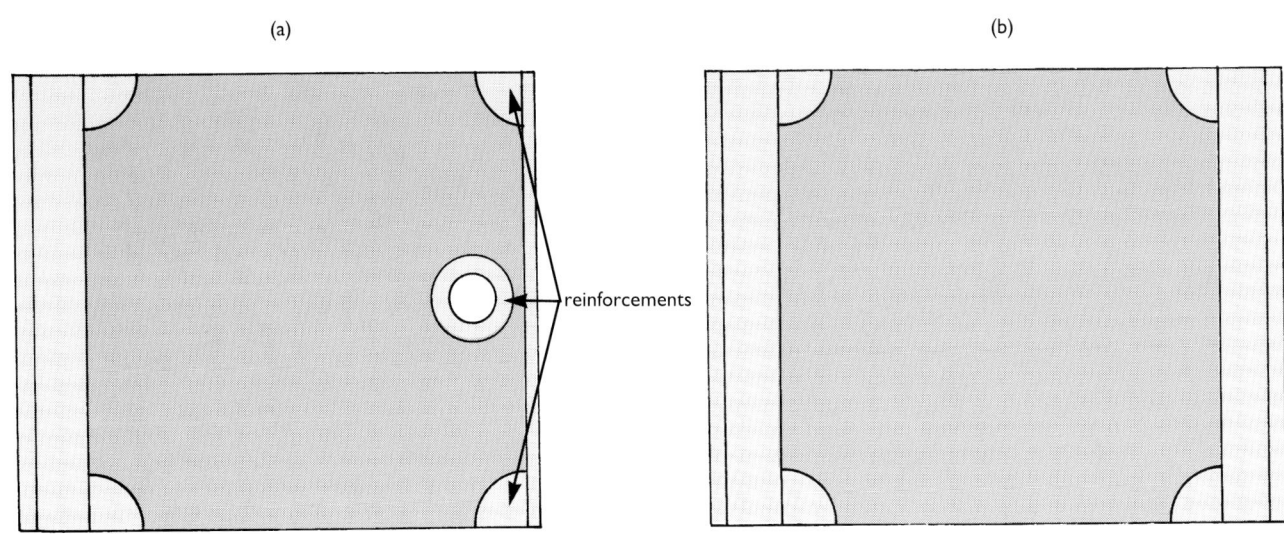

(a)

(b)

reinforcements

77 Completed panels: (a) upper panel (b) lower panel

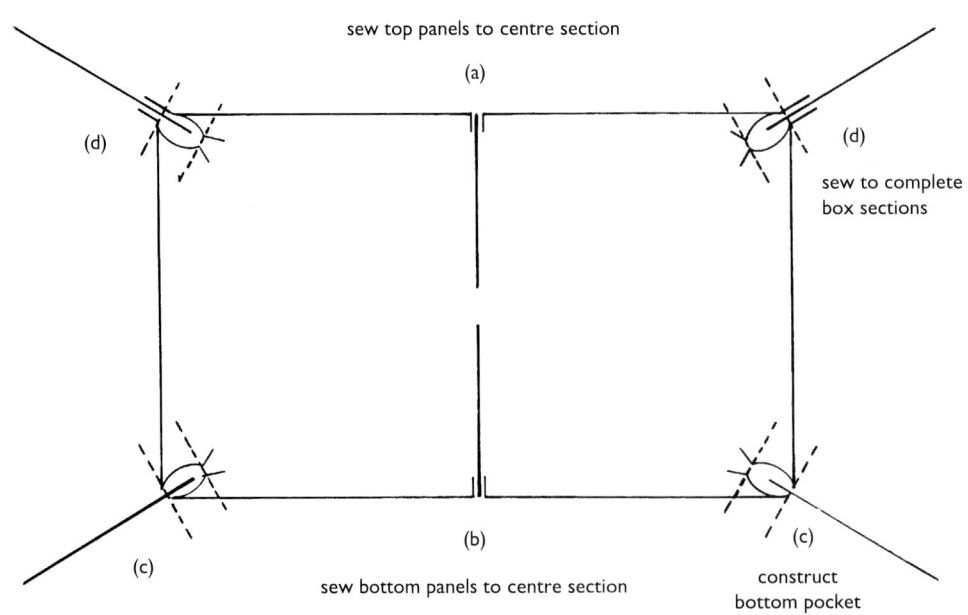

sew top panels to centre section

(a)

(d)

(d)

sew to complete box sections

(c)

(b)

(c)

sew bottom panels to centre section

construct bottom pocket

78 Assembly sequence for Cody war kite

LARGE CODY WAR KITE

One of the most attractive features of the Cody design is that it can be scaled up to produce large, extremely strong kites, as long as care is taken to reinforce the panels at stress points and to use more robust timber for the longerons and spars. The pockets will of course also need to be bigger to compensate for the larger spars. The materials below will produce a large war kite with the cells based on a unit size of 750 mm.

Note:

As an alternative to hardwood dowel, bamboo could be used as it is both light and strong, although it is difficult to find canes of good enough quality. The type sold in garden centres are invariably too uneven and brittle.

Sometimes large Cody kites utilize aluminium tube or fibreglass for the frame materials, but great care then has to be exercised when flying the kite, as a large kite sparred up with aluminium can cause substantial damage if control is lost. There would be major problems if the kite should hit power lines. A kite with metal spars will also appear on airport radars, which could cause safety problems.

MATERIALS

○ Fabric: ripstop nylon, 20 x 1 m
○ Longerons: hardwood dowel, six pieces 12 x 2350 mm
○ Front diagonals: hardwood dowel, two pieces 15 x 3500 mm
○ Rear diagonals: hardwood dowel, two pieces 15 x 2900 mm
○ Wing bracers: hardwood dowel, two pieces 9 x 900 mm
○ PVA adhesive
○ Plastic beads x 12
○ Line tensioners x 6
○ Aluminium ring for bridling point

Large Cody war kite

METHOD

The large war kite is basically made in the same way as the scaled-down model, but some extra work is involved.

1 At the fabrication stage, reinforcements are sewn to all the corners and other vulnerable points (Figure 79). Cut circles of ripstop 150 mm in diameter and fold them in half. Glue the halves together to produce a double-thickness semi-circular section. Cut this in half to make two corner-reinforcement pieces; glue these into the corners of the panel and stitch down. (Instead of circles, triangular pieces may be used.)

2 The centre panel of the larger Cody has spars at the top and bottom to give extra strength. Form the pockets to accommodate these spars from extra pocket allowances on the inner edges of the upper and lower panels (see Figure 77 on page 86).

3 Sew tape loops to the centre panel to provide attachment points for beads. These fit into notches in the end of the 9 mm spars, which in turn fit into the pockets.

4 The notch-and-bead system employed on the small Cody is adequate for locating the longerons, but is insufficient for the wing tensioning. At the bottom corners, form thick flying line (200 lb) into a loop

30 mm in length when pulled out. Tensioning is achieved using a tensioning system at the upper corner (see Figure 71 on page 83). Using this system it is possible to get good tension into the panels, which is essential for efficient flight.

5 A kite of this size will need to be flown on high-quality line with a breaking strain in the region of 200 kg (500 lb).

79 Reinforcement to upper wing and body

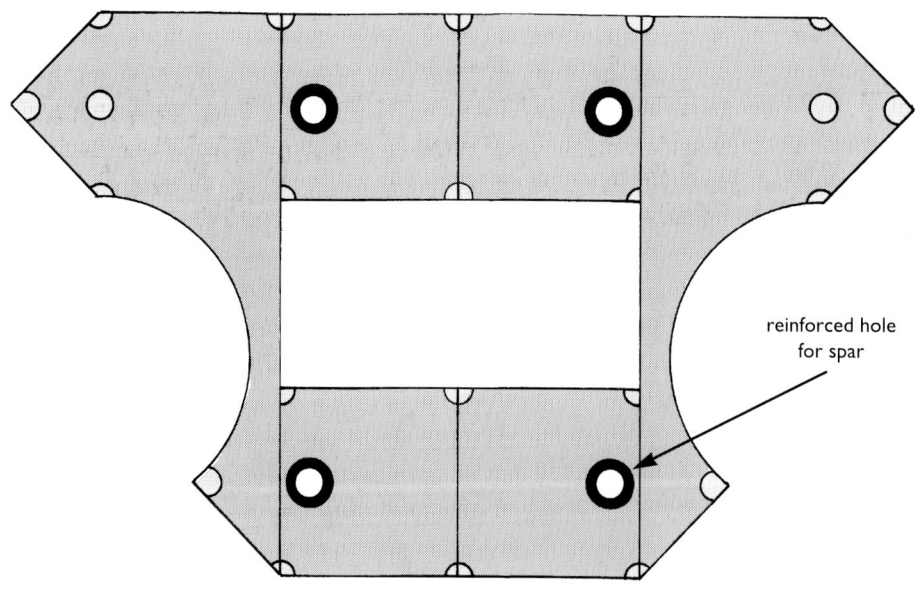

reinforced hole
for spar

EXTENDED-WING CODY

The larger wings of this variation give a greater degree of lift than a shorter-winged version with the same-sized box section. One of Cody's aims was to make a war kite which could be flown in very high winds, and it is possible that the reason he turned to the shorter-winged type was to fly kites in wind speeds of up to 70 miles per hour. The extended-wing Cody is a particularly nice kite to fly, and can be fitted with an additional upper wing if desired.

Extended-wing Cody

MATERIALS

○ Fabric: ripstop nylon or other suitable fabric, 7 x 1 m
○ Longerons: hardwood dowel, six pieces 9 x 1450 mm
○ Front diagonal spars: hardwood dowel, two pieces 12 x 2500 mm
○ Rear spars: hardwood dowel, two pieces 12 x 1600 mm
○ Outer-wing bracers: square hardwood, two pieces 6 x 6 x 550 mm
○ Inner-wing bracers: square hardwood, two pieces 6 x 6 x 700 mm
○ PVA adhesive
○ Plastic beads x 20
○ Aluminium ring for bridling point
○ Aluminium tube: internal diameter 9 mm, 2 x 50 mm lengths (to act as a joint for front diagonal spars)

METHOD

The extended-wing Cody is constructed in the same way as the war kites. The wing, however, is a more substantial structure which requires some additional work.

1   Cut out the main body of the wings (Figures 80 and 81) and attach the pointed sections at the end as before (page 81). The wing has one more panel than the standard Cody wing, and therefore needs an additional lateral pocket (see Figure 82).

2   Stitch a tape loop to the two pockets which are fitted to each wing (see Figure 70 on page 83) before fitting them to the underside of the wing; these will form additional points to support the wing.

3   Sew tape loops to the wing at the points where the pockets will terminate, and affix the pockets. The diagonal Cody spars will need to be supported and this can be done by sewing three tape loops on to the upper surface of the wings at the positions shown. Before fixing these tape loops, however, it is worth sewing a reinforcement patch to the wings. The competed wing section (upper surface) is shown in Figure 82.

4   Cut the panels (Figures 83–6) and sew the hems as appropriate. Mark the position of the holes through which the diagonals will pass, and either hot-cut with a soldering iron or cut with a sharp blade and sew around the edge. It is a good idea to sew a piece of reinforcing fabric around the area where the hole will be cut beforehand, to form a stronger hole.

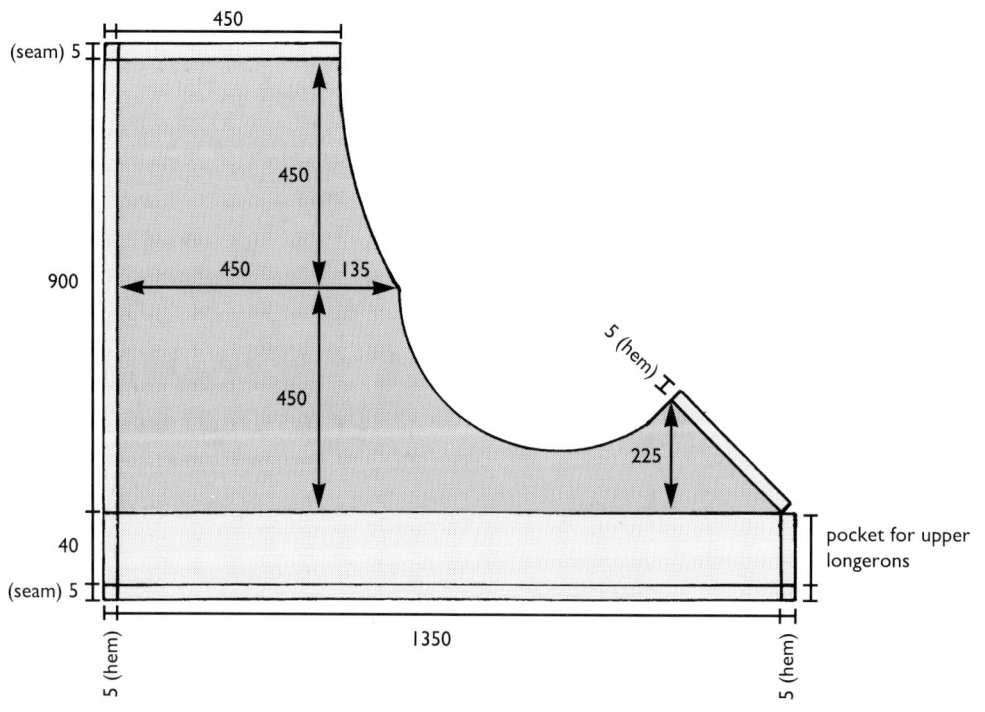

80   Marking pattern for wing x 2

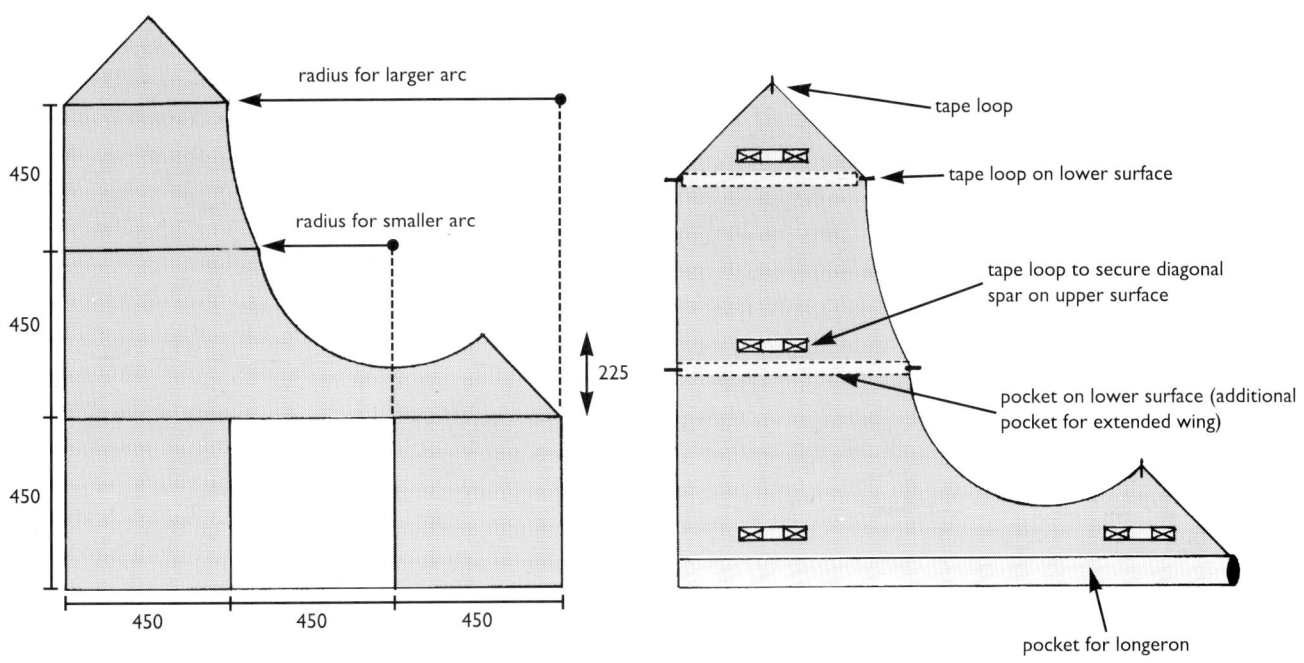

450

450

450

450

450

450

radius for larger arc

radius for smaller arc

225

**81 Marking pattern for wing
and upper surface**

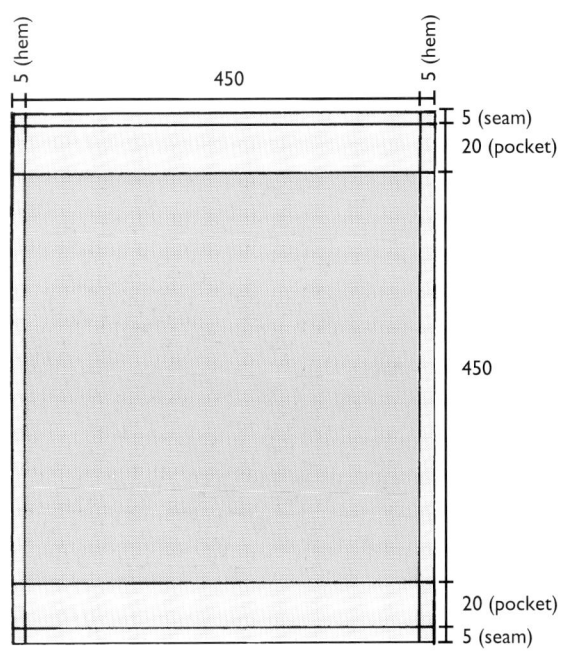

tape loop

tape loop on lower surface

tape loop to secure diagonal
spar on upper surface

pocket on lower surface (additional
pocket for extended wing)

pocket for longeron

**82   Completed wing section
(upper surface)**

450

5 (hem)

5 (hem)

5 (seam)

10
40

450

20 (pocket)

5 (seam)

**83   Marking pattern for upper
panel x 4**

5 (hem)

450

5 (hem)

5 (seam)
20 (pocket)

450

20 (pocket)

5 (seam)

**84   Marking pattern for lower
panel x 4**

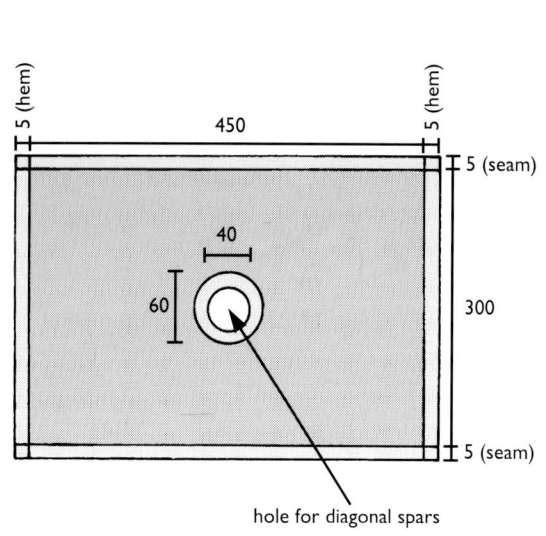

85 Marking pattern for centre panel x 2

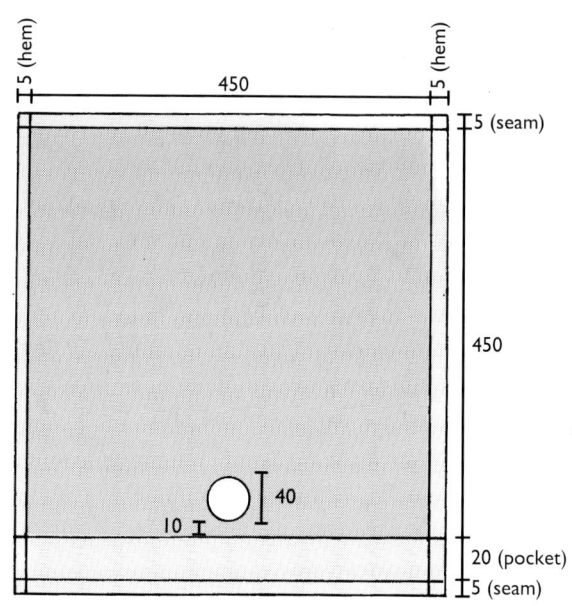

86 Marking pattern for side panel x 4

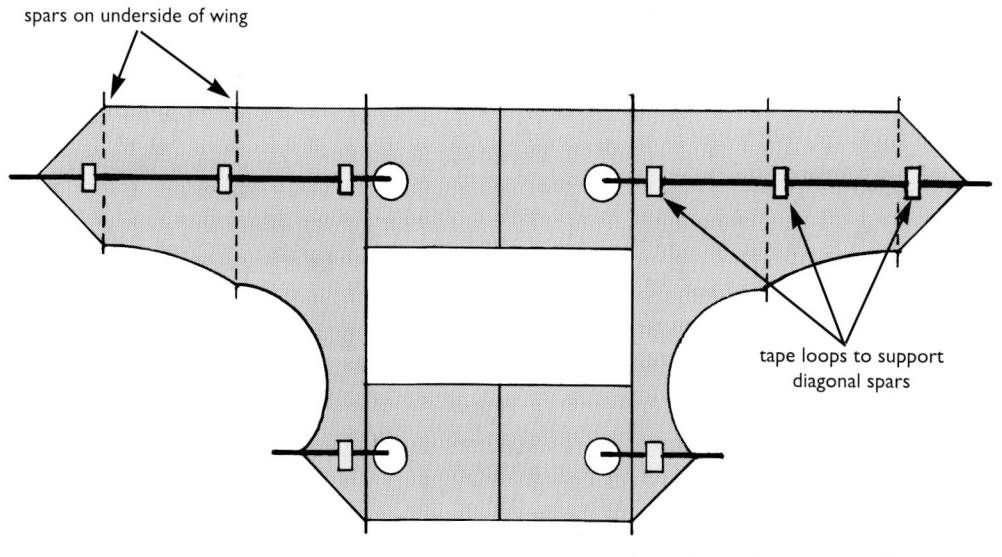

87 View of upper surface

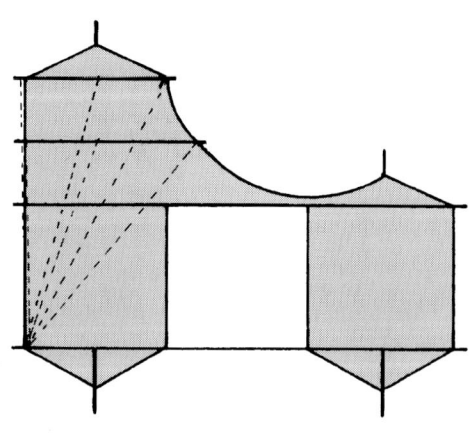

bracing lines run from the nose to the edges and centres of the wing bracers

88 Side elevation: the large wing is supported by a number of bracing lines

89 Bracing lines seen from the front of the kite

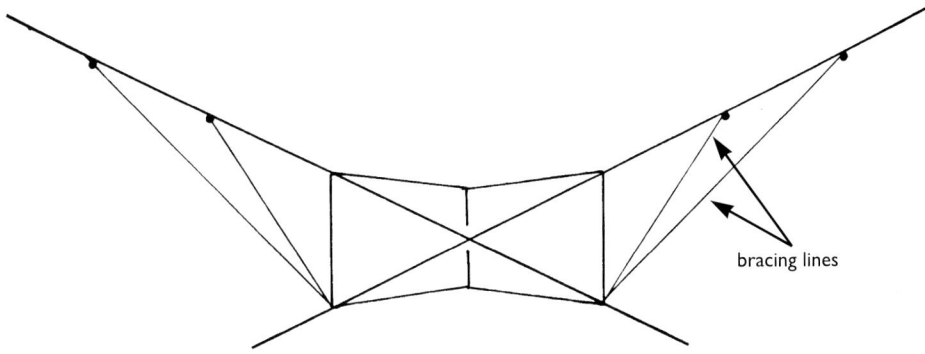

bracing lines

90 Attachment point for the flying line: front view

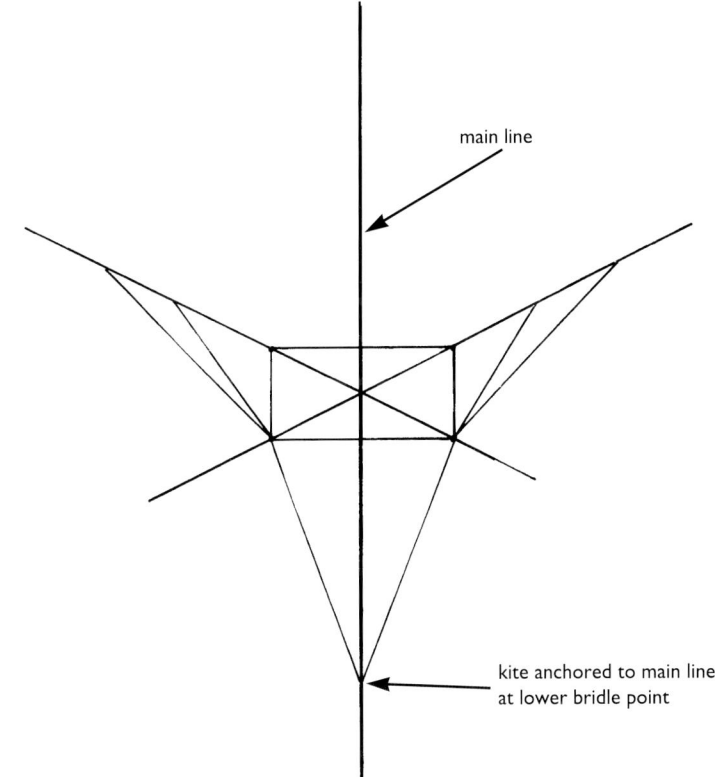

main line

kite anchored to main line at lower bridle point

5 Assemble the kite as with the large Cody (page 88), but cut the two longerons for the centre pockets the same length as those for the outer box sections to give the kite strength and rigidity. The completed kite (upper surface) is shown in Figure 87, and the bracing lines (side and front elevations) in Figures 88 and 89.

6 The flying-line attachment point is shown in Figure 90. The kite should be flown from 150 kg (300 lb) breaking-strain line.

FURTHER READING

Eden, M. *Kiteworks* (Sterling, 1989)

Greger, M. *Kites for Everyone* (M. Greger, import available at specialist kite shops, 1983)

Hart, C. *Kites: An Historical Survey* (Paul P. Appel, New York, second edition 1982)

Hunt, L. *Twenty-five Kites that Fly* (Bruce Publishing, Milwaukee, 1929; reprinted Dover Publications, New York, 1971)

Lee, A.G. *The Flying Cathedral: The Story of S.F. Cody* (Methuen, 1965)

Moulton, R. *Kites* (Pelham, 1978)

Pelham, D. *Penguin Book of Kites* (Penguin, 1977)

Rowlands, J. *Kites and Windsocks* (B.T. Batsford, 1992)

Rowlands, J. *Kites to Make and Fly* (B.T. Batsford, 1989)

Rowlands, J. *Making and Flying Modern Kites* (B.T. Batsford, 1989)

Schimmelpfennig, W. *Making and Flying Kites* (Hamlyn, 1988)

Shaw, W.H. and Ruhen, O. *Lawrence Hargrave: Explorer, Inventor and Aviation Experimenter* (Cassell, Australia, 1977)

Walker, P.B. *Early Aviation at Farnborough. Vol. 1: Balloons, Kites and Airships* (Macdonald, 1971)

USEFUL ADDRESSES

SUPPLIERS

Bristol Kite Store
1b Pitville Place
Cotham Hill
Bristol BS6 6JY
Tel: 0272-745010

Kiteability
(Mail order only)
2 Garfield Road
Enfield EN3 4RP
Tel: 081-804 9080

Malvern Kites
Unicorn Yard
Great Malvern
Worcestershire WR14 4PZ
Tel: 0684-565504

The Kite Store
28 Neal Street
London WC2H 9PA
Tel: 071-836 1666

Windthings
11 Cowgatehead
Edinburgh EH1 1JY
Tel: 031-220 6336

KITING ORGANIZATIONS

UK

The Kite Society of Great Britain
31 Grange Road
Ilford
Essex IG1 1EU

USA

American Kitefliers' Association
1559 Rockville Pike
Rockville
Maryland 20852

Kitelines
PO Box 466
Randallstown
Maryland 21133-0466

INDEX

Aerocurve kite 7
Anatomy of a box kite 14

Barrage kites 10-11
Beauford scale 16
Bell, Alexander Graham 6-7, 41
Bell's tetrahedral kite *41*
Box Delta 71-4, *71*
Bridling 33-4

Cellular kites 12
Centre of pressure 18-20
Cody, Samuel Franklyn 8-9
Cody train *15*
Cody war kite *20*, 78-86, *78*
    extended-wing 89-93
    large 87-8
Compound designs 67-93
    box delta 71-4
    Cody war kite 78-86
    extended-wing Cody 89-93
    large Cody war kite 87-8
    three-celled winged box kite 75-7
    winged box kite 68-70
Conyne kite *1*, 52-4, *52*

Decorative techniques 27
Delta Conyne *16*
Dice kite 38-40, *38*
Drag 17

Eight-unit Waldorf assembly kite *19*
Extended-wing Cody 89-93, *89*

Facet kites 12
Flexifoil 12
Flying line 26
Franklin, Benjamin 10
French rescue kite 55-7, *55*
French signal kite 52

Gravity 17

Hargrave box kite 44-6, *44*
Hargrave, Lawrence 6-7, 14

Knots *27-8*

Lamson, Charles J. 7
Large Cody war kite 87-8, *87*
Lift 17, 19-20

Man-lifters 8-9
Materials 21-8
Meteorological research 9, 10

Novelty kites 12

Parafoils 12, *12*
Peter Lynn Tri-D box kite 63-6, *63*

Rainbow kite 35-7, *35*

Sail materials 22-5
    cloth 22
    polyester film 24
    polythene 23
    ripstop nylon 22
Saul's naval barrage kite 47-50, *47*
Simple box kite made from fabric *30*, 33-4
Simple box kite made from hardwood and plastic sheeting 30-2
Simple box kites 29-50
    dice 38-40
    Hargrave 44-6
    made from fabric 33-4
    made from hardwood and plastic sheeting 30-2
    rainbow 35-7
    Saul's naval barrage kite 47-50
    single-celled tetrahedron made from

bamboo and plastic sheeting 41-2
single-celled tetrahedron made from ripstop nylon 43
Single-celled tetrahedron made from bamboo and plastic sheeting 41-2
Single-celled tetrahedron made from ripstop nylon 43, *43*
Spars 24-5
    aluminium alloy 25
    bamboo 25
    carbon fibre 25
    fibreglass 25
    hardwood 25
Stability 18-20
Sutton Flowform *15*

Thermoplastic tubing for joints *31*
Three-celled winged box kite 75-7, *75*
Train kite *17*
Triple-stack Delta Conyne 58-62, *58*

War kites 8-9
Wind 15-20
    Beauford scale 16
    centre of pressure 18-20
    drag 17
    gravity 17
    ground turbulence 16
    lift 17, 19-20
    quality 15
    speed 15
Winerack kite *15*
Winged box kite 68-70, *68*
Winged box kites 51-66
    Conyne 52-4
    French rescue kite 55-7
    Peter Lynn Tri-D box kite 63-6
    triple-stack Delta Conyne 58-62
Wright brothers 9